AN **INTRODUCTION** TO
SETTLEMENT GEOGRAPHY

William F. Hornby

Formerly Principal Lecturer in Geography
Sheffield City Polytechnic

Melvyn Jones

Senior Lecturer in Geography
Sheffield City Polytechnic

PUBLISHED BY THE PRESS SYNDICATE OF THE UNIVERSITY OF CAMBRIDGE
The Pitt Building, Trumpington Street, Cambridge, United Kingdom

CAMBRIDGE UNIVERSITY PRESS
The Edinburgh Building, Cambridge CB2 2RU, UK
40 West 20th Street, New York, NY 10011–4211, USA
10 Stamford Road, Oakleigh, VIC 3166, Australia
Ruiz de Alarcón 13, 28014 Madrid, Spain
Dock House, The Waterfront, Cape Town 8001, South Africa

http://www.cambridge.org

First published 1991
Fourth printing 2001

Printed in the United Kingdom at the University Press, Cambridge

British Library Cataloguing in Publication data
Hornby, William F. (William Fredric) 1934–
    An introduction to settlement geography.
    1. Human settlement. Geographical aspects
    I. Title II. Jones, Melvyn III. Series
    910.09173

ISBN 0 521 28263 2 paperback

ACKNOWLEDGEMENTS
The publishers would like to thank the following for permission to
reproduce the photographs, diagrams and extracts: The Institute of
British Geographers for the extract on p. 1, from A. E. Smailes (1971)
'Urban Systems', *Transactions of the Institute of British Geographers*
53, p. 7, and for Figs 5.3 and 5.4, from A. E. Smailes (1964) 'Some
reflections on the geographical description and analysis of townscapes',
TIBG 21, pp. 99–115; the *Geographical Journal* for the extract on p.4,
from A. G. Champion (1989) 'Counterurbanisation in Britain',
Geographical Journal 155, pp. 52–53; University of Cambridge
Committee of Aerial Photography for Fig. 2.6; Longman Group UK Ltd
for Fig. 2.7, from B. K. Roberts (1987) *The Making of the English
Village*; World Publications Ltd for Fig. 3.5, from R. Ghate (1978)
'Generation gap in an Indian village', *Geographical Magazine* 50, pp.
580–86; Richardsons Developments Ltd for Fig. 8.10; and the United
Nations for Fig. 8.12.

Every effort has been made to reach copyright holders; the publishers
would be glad to hear from anyone whose rights they have unknowingly
infringed.

All photographs except for Figs 2.6 and 8.12 are the authors'.

Designed and produced by The Pen & Ink Book Company Ltd,
Huntingdon, Cambridgeshire

Contents

Exercises and Case Studies

Exercises

Case Studies

1

Introduction

Rural and urban settlement studies

The problem of defining 'rural' and 'urban' settlements has long interested geographers though increasingly it has been recognised that attempts to make a strong distinction between the two tend to create more problems than they solve. The two main perceptions of 'rural' and 'urban' are of sociological origin. One views rural and urban as two poles of a rural–urban dichotomy; the other views the rural–urban issue as a continuum in which clear distinctions can be made between the two extremes but where there is increased blurring towards the middle. With the high levels of mobility associated with modern lifestyles and the increased interaction between rural and urban areas, however defined, the concept of a continuum tends to be more representative of the real world situation in which both rural and urban dwellers live. It does, however, suggest that there are degrees of 'rurality' and 'urban-ness' from what one researcher (Cloke, 1977), attempting to 'pin down the nebulous concept of rurality' in England and Wales, has called 'extreme rurality' on the one hand to 'extreme non-rurality' on the other (see Chapter 2). Smailes' (1971) description of areas that would fall into the latter category, clearly emphasises the interactions between urban areas and some rural areas.

> Here the countryside, long subject to urban needs, is occupied increasingly by families of urban origin. It is long since farmers were in the majority, yet most of the area remains farmland. This farmland is now operated by a small, well-equipped personnel – probably not more than 2 per cent of the resident population are farmers. Villages in the sociological sense of the term, communities, the majority of whose workers are engaged in agriculture, are no longer to be found. The observant traveller will notice as conspicuous features in the so-called villages and hamlets, as well as along the roads that

interconnect the urban nodes, many pointers to the penetration of urban influence and the gearing of the economy to the needs of town dwellers. Numerous catering facilities, for food as well as drink, garden centres for stocking suburban gardens, roadside advertisement and vending of fresh foods that are produced locally, boarding kennels as well as breeding and trimming kennels for towndwellers' pets, are all evidences of the intensity of the frequenting of the countryside by town-folk and their impact on its life.

Obviously the degree of penetration of the countryside by urban influences varies between different parts of the world as well as within individual countries. Increasingly, however, such influences are having an effect on rural ways of life in the developing countries in Latin America, Asia and Africa just as they have done in more developed nations. Rural–urban migration in many developing countries has reached unprecedented levels since 1950 but the traffic in people, ideas and skills has not all been one-way. There have been important 'backwash' effects on rural communities in such areas generated largely by returning migrants with varying urban experiences and outlooks. Thus interaction between rural and urban areas is of major significance in both developed and developing countries and is likely to continue to grow in the foreseeable future, further blurring the differences between many such areas.

Urbanisation, suburbanisation and counterurbanisation

From the introductory comments already made, it is clear that any study of settlement geography must inevitably take account of the dynamic nature of the subject. Settlements do not remain unchanged. They are affected by a multitude of influences that encourage changes in their morphology and their social and economic geography. During the past 200 years or so, major economic and demographic changes in the world have been fundamental to settlement changes on an unprecedented scale. General shifts in population between urban and rural areas can be identified at different stages of this period, and it is helpful to outline these briefly as they are basic to many aspects of settlement change. The process of urbanisation (the concentration of people into urban areas) has been the most dramatic of these population shifts.

Urbanisation

As recently as 1800 only some 3 per cent of the world's people lived in settlements with a population of more than 5,000. By 1900, this proportion had increased four- or five-fold and by the year 2000 it is anticipated that well over half the world's population of more than 6,000 million will be living in urban settlements. Many of these people will be in 'million cities' (settlements of over 1 million inhabitants) and according to some population projections there may by then be as many as 20 cities each with a population in excess of 10 million. Mountjoy (1986) has traced the growth of million cities from the early 1920s to the early 1980s (Fig. 1.1), emphasising the increase in the total number of such cities, the increasing concentration of million cities in lower latitudes (many of

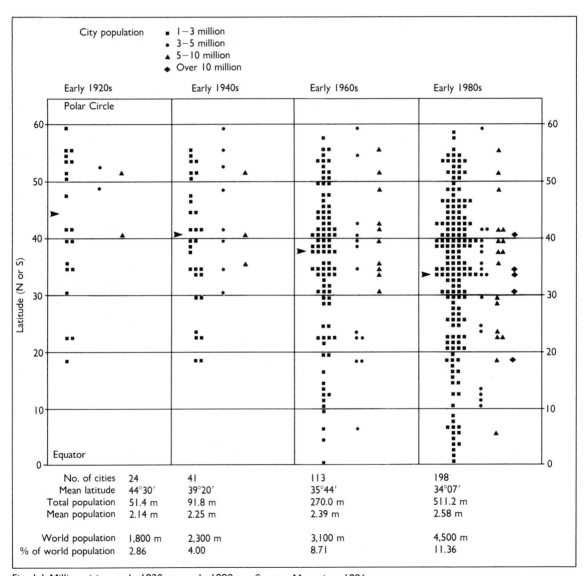

Fig. 1.1 Million cities: early 1920s to early 1980s.   *Source*: Mountjoy, 1986.

them in developing countries), and the recent development of what he calls 'mega-cities' of over 10 million people.

Comparison of the levels of urbanisation (the proportion of the total population living in urban areas, usually expressed as a percentage) in different countries is difficult because the definition of 'urban areas' varies greatly and has also changed through time. Nevertheless it is clear that between 1750 and 1950 urbanisation was most marked in the developed countries. Largely associated with industrialisation, urbanisation was a response to the quickening of rates of economic growth and the need for a centralised factory labour force and related service sector, resulting in rural–urban migration and rapid changes in the morphology and socio-economic geography of urban areas. More recently, urbanisation has been dominated by the growth of cities in the developing countries of Latin America, Asia and Africa. Already several developing countries, mainly in Latin America, have urbanisation levels comparable with those of most developed countries. From a situation in which in 1950 just over one-third of the world's population living in urban areas of over 20,000 were in developing countries, by the year 2000 it is anticipated that almost two-thirds of the world's urban population will be in such countries. By then, according to UN projections,

Mexico City could have a population of 31 million, São Paulo in Brazil 26 million and the Chinese cities, Shanghai and Beijing, over 20 million each. The growth in urban population in many developing countries has already had an enormous impact on the geography of urban settlements and, as much of the increase is related to rural–urban migration, it clearly also reflects and influences change in rural communities.

Suburbanisation

As cities increased in population during the 19th and early 20th centuries, physical expansion of the urban built-up area also occurred. Rapid outward growth, in Europe and North America especially, was facilitated by public transport developments, with farms, hamlets and villages being engulfed by the outward growth of suburban areas. The inhabitants of such areas were able to commute to work in the city centres, at first by rail and later also by tram or bus. From the early stages of railway development some villages beyond the immediate built-up area of the cities also underwent a process of 'suburbanisation', as it became possible for people to live in such settlements and commute to work in the cities in a relatively short time.

Much greater development of the suburbanisation process occurred in developed countries after the Second World War. Increasing affluence, efficient public transportation and dramatic increases in private car ownership made it possible for many more people to choose to live in settlements that could still be perceived as rural, although the majority of the residents commuted to towns for work, recreation and many of the goods and services they required. Such settlements have been given a variety of names, for example dormitory villages, suburbanised villages, commuter settlements, discontinuous suburbs and metropolitan villages. The development of these settlements has inevitably been accompanied by major changes in their morphology and in their social and economic structure that have proved of considerable interest to geographers. The process of suburbanisation, whether viewed in terms of the growth of cities through the movement of population into suburban areas within the cities themselves, or as the suburbanisation of settlements physically separated from the urban

Exercise 1.1

World million cities

Examine Fig. 1.1 which shows million cities at different dates between the early 1920s and the early 1980s.

a) Describe the changes indicated in the diagram in terms of:
   i) the total number of million cities in each of the categories indicated in the key; and
   ii) the distribution of such cities in relation to latitude.

b) Discuss possible reasons for and implications of the changes you have described. (At this stage your discussion may be at a fairly general level. It should prove useful to return to this discussion at a later stage of your studies.)

built-up area (sometimes called 'extended' suburbanisation), represents a significant trend in the re-distribution of population away from city centres. The many pressures imposed on settlements outside the urban built-up area but within daily commuter access to the city have led to the concept of such areas as 'pressured' rural areas (Cloke, 1979) in contrast to 'remote' rural areas that, initially at least, seemed little affected by the dispersal of residential population from urban areas. In the United Kingdom, many of these remote areas continued to be subject to depopulation in the 1950s and 1960s while pressured rural areas were showing substantial population gains.

Counterurbanisation

However, by the 1970s, clear evidence was emerging of population increases in most of these more remote rural areas (Fig. 1.2) and this pattern of population increase in settlements beyond the daily commuter range of urban centres has also been observed in other parts of Europe, North America and other developed regions, in some cases perhaps beginning rather earlier than in the UK. Certain writers began to differentiate between the suburbanisation or extended suburbanisation process relating to settlements within daily commuter range of urban centres and a counterurbanisation process that was related to population growth in rural areas beyond the limits of the daily urban commuter system. Others saw counterurbanisation as including both these processes of population growth in non-urban areas. Yet others have suggested that terms like 'rural regeneration' or 'rural resurgence' might be more appropriate ways of acknowledging the fact that population growth is now occurring in different kinds of rural areas in developed countries and that the reasons for this may be related to rural-centred factors of change rather than solely urban-based influences.

As Champion (1989) has suggested, it is perhaps helpful to adopt a working definition of 'counterurbanisation' that can be refined in due course when further evidence is available.

Just as in geographical terms urbanisation involved the increasing concentration of population into larger and more densely occupied settlements, so counterurbanisation

represents a shift in the reverse direction, with the redistribution of population from major cities and metropolitan concentrations towards smaller metropolitan areas and beyond into non-metropolitan territory. This signifies a switch from concentration to dispersal, from shifts in overall population distribution up the urban hierarchy to shifts down the settlement-size gradient, and from a less even to a more even spread of population over geographical space.

This working definition would include suburbanisation (or extended suburbanisation) as part of the wider counterurbanisation process without necessarily excluding use of the term to describe the more limited features to which it directly relates.

Urbanisation, suburbanisation and counterurbanisation processes have had major influences on settlements in developed countries. In developing countries, attention is still largely focused on the striking growth in urbanisation, although suburbanisation is clearly evident in many major city-regions. Counterurbanisation in developing countries is, as yet, a feature apparent only in a few special cases (for example in some growing resort areas and some planned rural development schemes). It will be interesting to see to what extent the experience of developed countries is followed in Asia, Africa and Latin America in the future.

Exercise 1.2

Urban and rural population change in Great Britain, 1971–81

Examine Fig. 1.2 which shows population change in Great Britain between 1971 and 1981.

a) Describe the general patterns of population gains and losses apparent from the map in relation to the kinds of area in which they occurred.

b) Suggest to what extent these patterns can be related to the processes of urbanisation, suburbanisation and counterurbanisation.

Fig. 1.2 Population change in Great Britain by Economic Planning Region, 1971–81.
Source: Office of Population Censuses and Surveys.   ▶

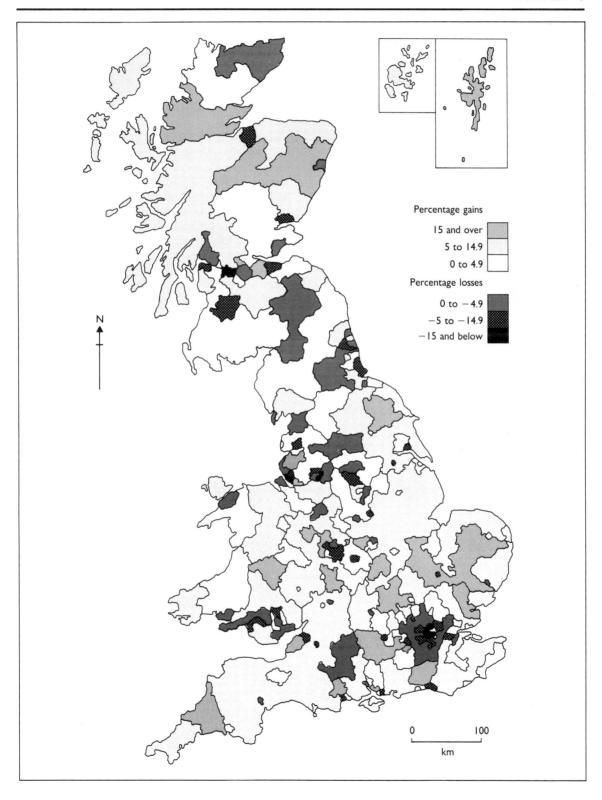

Percentage gains

15 and over

5 to 14.9

0 to 4.9

Percentage losses

0 to −4.9

−5 to −14.9

−15 and below

N

0   100

km

Organisation of this book

The content and structure of this book are designed to focus on the changing concerns of urban and rural geography largely brought about by the major processes outlined in the preceding section. As already indicated, it is not always easy to differentiate clearly between rural and urban issues in settlement studies and inevitably such issues will overlap in some cases. Nevertheless, it was thought that it would be helpful for students using this book to deal first with rural and then with urban settlements. It is therefore divided into two main sections concerned respectively with rural settlement issues and urban settlement issues. The first section deals with rural settlement patterns and forms, the socio-economic geography of rural settlements, and rural settlement planning. The second part is concerned with urban morph-

ology, the social geography of urban areas, housing and residential mobility in urban areas, the economic geography of urban areas, and urban settlement planning.

Within each chapter, the general examination of the theme is accompanied by a detailed case study or studies selected from contrasting areas. This reflects the need for students to have both a general knowledge of a broad field of study and a detailed knowledge of specific cases. Each case study is concerned with the exemplification of selected concepts, models or themes in the setting of the particular area. To help students to achieve a fuller understanding of many of the concepts introduced in the text, exercises are also included in each chapter. These are mainly of the data response type and should help students to develop interpretive and analytical skills.

2

Rural settlement patterns and forms

Traditionally, geographers studying rural settlements have focused mainly on the origins and evolution of such settlements and on their spatial patterns both in relation to one another and within individual settlements. More recently, there has been an increased interest in the social geography of rural areas, This, at least in part, is related to the greater social and economic complexity of such areas that has resulted from urban industrialisation, agricultural modernisation and the increased mobility of the many people who now choose to live in the countryside, though not involved in traditional rural occupations.

What is 'rural'?

As suggested in Chapter 1, recent changes have led to a blurring of the distinctions between rural and urban areas. Various writers have attempted to distinguish between such areas using indicators such as population density, land use, employment types, commuting patterns, visual appearance and distance from large centres of population.

Cloke (1979) adopted a fairly sophisticated approach to determine an 'index of rurality' using 16 variables based largely on census data for each rural district in England and Wales in 1961. On the basis of this he recognised four categories of rural area ranging from 'extreme rural' through 'intermediate rural' and 'intermediate non-rural' to 'extreme non-rural'. Four major zones of 'extreme rural' areas emerged from his analysis: the south-west peninsula; Wales and its borderlands (excluding the industrial areas of the south and north-east); Norfolk, north Suffolk and the Wash area of Lincolnshire; and a discontinuous belt of the northern Pennines. Cloke has since applied a similar analysis following subsequent censuses in England and Wales, though direct comparisons are difficult because of the changing nature of census data at different censuses. Nevertheless, a fairly similar pattern has been revealed at each census — albeit with sufficient variations to emphasise that 'rurality' is far from being a static feature. It is also important to remember that the weighting given to different indicators has an important bearing on the final index for each area. Cloke's approach clearly emphasises the difficulties involved in attempting to identify precisely what is meant by 'rural'.

In this book, a broad view is taken of the term in keeping with the ideas of writers such as Wibberley (1972) who saw 'rural' as a term describing 'those parts of a country which show unmistakable signs of being dominated by extensive uses of land, either at the present time or in the immediate past'. Although a broad definition of this kind is far from perfect, it enables an investigation of 'settlements which to the eye still appear to be rural but which, in practice, are merely an extension of the city resulting from the development of the commuter train and the private motor car'. It also has the advantage of being suitable for use on an international basis.

Rural settlement patterns

Most studies of rural settlement pattern and form distinguish two basic types of settlement: those that are *clustered* and those that are *dispersed*. As in many other aspects of geographical study, problems may arise from the terminology used by different writers. In particular, in this context the term 'nucleated' may be used rather than 'clustered' but in an attempt to avoid confusion with our later discussion of village form we have confined the use of the term 'nucleated' to descriptions of the form of particular villages rather than used it to describe overall settlement patterns.

Clustered and dispersed settlement patterns

In their simplest traditional form these two types of settlement pattern are represented on the one hand by a village whose inhabitants live in a tightly clustered central location and farm the area surrounding this and, on the other hand, by a scatter of farmsteads, each of which is located within the farmland worked by its occupants. Obviously there are many variations from such a simple model, with a range of patterns varying from extreme clustering to extreme dispersal, through a host of intermediate types.

The attempt by Thorpe (1964) to classify rural settlements in Britain and map their distribution (Fig. 2.1) illustrates some of the problems of such an exercise. Thorpe defined a hamlet as a nucleated settlement, with or without a parish church, having from 3 to 19 homesteads, whereas a village was seen as a nucleated rural settlement of 20 or more households, differentiated from a small market town by the limited range and number of its services. The classification thus used not only settlement size but also function in an attempt to differentiate between settlements.

However, it clearly raises many questions in a situation where there is no clear-cut break in the continuum of population size of hamlets and villages and no very obvious pattern of associated services differentiating large villages from small towns. In many parts of the world the situation is further complicated by such factors as the presence of temporary as well as permanent settlements (for example where pastoral nomadism is practised by some of the population), or the super-imposition of one culture on another, as in many former colonial territories.

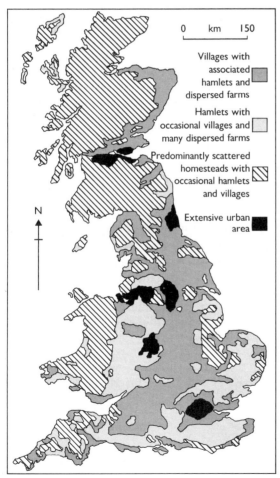

Fig. 2.1 The distribution of rural settlement types in Britain.
Source: Thorpe, 1964.

Nearest neighbour analysis

In recent years, considerable attention has been devoted to attempts to describe patterns of settlement based on the technique of nearest neighbour analysis. This technique, 'borrowed' from plant ecologists, considers the location of individual points (in this case, rural settlements) in relation to other similar points in an area. It is an approach designed to provide a more objective, statistically based method of describing settlement distributions. The technique involves calculation of a *nearest neighbour index (Rn)* based on a comparison between the settlement pattern actually observed in an area and an assumed random settlement pattern. In theory the index can range from 0 (when all points are clustered closely together) to 2.15 (when all points are distributed uniformly throughout the area under consideration and so are as far away from one another as possible). An index value of 1.0 indicates a random distribution, while indices close to 0 are regarded as indicating a 'clustered' pattern, and those near to 2.15 a 'regular' pattern. Exercise 2.1 provides an illustration of how this approach can be used.

Though frequently advocated as a useful tool in the study of settlement patterns, the use of the nearest neighbour index has many limitations and can be misleading. Some of the main criticisms are as follows.

1   Radically different patterns of settlement may give rise to similar nearest neighbour indices. Figure 2.2 shows three contrasting patterns. The first, (a), is generated by random numbers and also provides a pattern of distribution which might well be described as 'random'. The other two patterns, (b) and (c), on a purely visual basis might be described as 'clustered' and 'regular' respectively. However, on the basis of nearest neighbour analysis they, like the pattern in (a), yield an index of 1.0 which suggests that all three are 'random' patterns. The nearest neighbour index has been claimed to avoid the vagueness and inaccuracy of merely verbal descriptions, but evidence of this kind obviously casts doubt on such claims.

2   Because only the *nearest* neighbour is used in calculations, the index only examines one aspect of settlement distribution and this may be misleading. For example, a pattern of closely 'paired' settlements at crossing points along a river would give an index very similar to that provided by many settlements close together; that is, both would have an index

close to 0. In normal terminology and understanding the first of these two situations would be unlikely to be seen as 'clustering' yet the index suggests that 'clustering' exists. Obviously if the *second* nearest neighbour was used for purposes of calculation, the two situations would be shown to be different, but such refinements are not usual – and, indeed, might lead to other problems of interpretation.

3   The choice of area is crucial in at least two ways. First, especially if a large area is chosen, the patterns in one part of an area may be 'averaged out' by contrasting patterns in another part of the area to provide an index near to 1.0 and give a false impression of 'randomness'. Second, a pattern that is 'clustered' (has an index near 0) at one scale, may be 'regular' (with an index near 2.15) at a larger scale.

4   The use of the term 'random' in this context may easily be taken to imply a chance distribution of settlement, though this may well not be the case in actuality.

Clearly there are many possible pitfalls in the use of this method of investigating settlement patterns. If used at all – and some would suggest it is better *not* to use it – it must be applied with great care and with an awareness of possible misleading interpretations. Additionally, it clearly does not provide any explanation of settlement patterns. This requires detailed investigation of a variety of factors.

Fig. 2.2 Nearest neighbour analysis. The diagrams indicate one of the problems associated with nearest neighbour analysis. The pattern in (a) was generated by random numbers, that in (b) might normally be described as 'clustered' and that in (c) as 'regular', but all yield a nearest neighbour index of 1.0.
Source: Dawson, 1975.

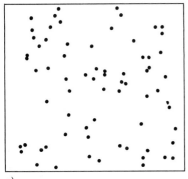

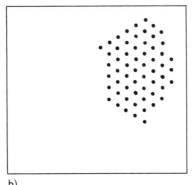

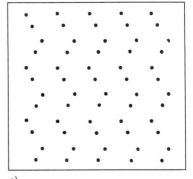

a)   b)   c)

Exercise 2.1

Nearest neighbour analysis

The formula for calculating the index is as follows:

$$Rn = \frac{D\,(obs)}{D\,(ran)} \quad \text{where}$$

Rn   is the nearest neighbour statistic;

D (obs) is the mean of the distances between the settlements in an area and the nearest neighbour of each of these settlements;

D (ran) is the assumed mean distance between settlements and their nearest neighbours if all the settlements were randomly distributed.

Apply the formula in a particular situation using the following procedure:

1 Delimit the area of study and define the type of settlements to be studied (not always an easy task – a group discussion on this may be helpful).

2 Locate the settlements in the pattern to be analysed on an appropriate map.

3 Measure the distance between each settlement and its nearest neighbour (the settlement closest to it) and record these distances.

4 Calculate the mean of the distances recorded in stage 3 above (D (obs) in the formula).

5 Calculate the expected mean distance between settlements and their nearest neighbours in a random distribution D (ran). This can be shown to be

$$0.5 \sqrt{\frac{a}{n}} \quad \text{where}$$

a = the area of study in km^2; and
n = the number of settlements within it.

6 Finally, calculate the nearest neighbour index using the formula:

$$Rn = \frac{D\,(obs)}{D\,(ran)}$$

Thus, if the mean distance between settlements in an area of 800 km^2 was 3.5 km and there were 25 settlements in the area:

a) the value of D (obs) would be 3.5;

b) the value of D (ran) would be $0.5\sqrt{\dfrac{800}{25}}$

$$= 0.5\,\sqrt{32} = 2.8;$$

c) the nearest neighbour index (Rn) could then be calculated

$$Rn = \frac{D\,(obs)}{D(ran)} = \frac{3.5}{2.8} = 1.25.$$

Critically discuss the value of your findings and the effectiveness of nearest neighbour analysis as a technique for describing settlement patterns.

Factors affecting settlement location and development

Present patterns of settlement represent just one stage in a continuing process that, in most parts of the world, began many centuries ago. It would seem reasonable to assume that most of the present settlement sites in rural areas of England were initially populated by individuals and groups who largely provided for their basic needs from their immediate locality, though probably having some links with neighbouring settlements. Chisholm (1968) has suggested that the Anglo-Saxons who settled much of England from about AD450 would have been chiefly concerned with the availability of water, arable land, grazing land, fuel and building materials, though there might be other important considerations such as defence and the need to avoid areas liable to periodic flooding. He argues that distance between resources and the settlement site is important and that hypothetical values can be placed on resources related to the concept of the basic cost to a community of being distanced from these resources. His ideas are summarised in Fig. 2.3. It is perhaps worth emphasising that most (perhaps almost all) of the settlements originally established by the Anglo-Saxons were small, and that recent evidence suggests – contrary to the general view when Chisholm was writing – that nucleated villages mainly developed after AD1000, possibly in many cases

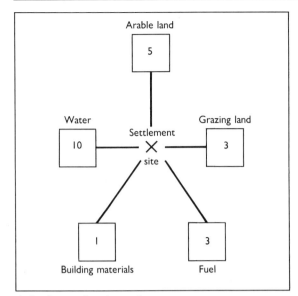

a) Settlement location and resources.

A	B Distance from settlement (km)		C Units of cost/km from settlement	D Product of B × C	
Resource	*x*	*y*		*x*	*y*
Water	0.1	0.5	10	1.0	5.0
Arable land	2.0	1.0	5	10.0	5.0
Grazing land	2.5	1.5	3	7.5	4.5
Fuel	2.5	2.0	3	7.5	6.0
Building materials	3.0	2.0	1	3.0	2.0
				29.0	22.5

b) Two hypothetical settlement locations.

Fig. 2.3 Settlement location in relation to resources. The values assigned to the different resources by Chisholm in (a) suggest that the removal of water over a set distance (say 1 km) from the settlement can be equated to 10 units of cost, but if the source of building materials is also 1 km from the settlement, this would represent only 1 unit of cost to the inhabitants. Chisholm places such a high value on water because of its use at frequent intervals and the difficulty of transporting it or storing it in large quantities in a fairly primitive society. Similarly, proximity to arable land is seen as being more valuable than nearness to grazing land because of the need for higher labour inputs on the arable land and for more frequent transport of goods to and from the fields.

In (b) Chisholm indicates how two alternative sites, *x* and *y*, might have been evaluated by people selecting a site for settlement, though obviously, in reality, the situation might be much less clear-cut. The availability of resources would be more varied than the model suggests – some might have potential for more than one type of use (e.g. arable or grazing), and the appreciation of the possibilities by the settlers was often perhaps insufficient to make rational judgements possible even on a qualitative basis. No doubt many mistakes were made and many compromises needed in these early days. *Source*: Chisholm, 1968.

in Midland England as the open-field system, characteristic of much medieval farming, developed with agricultural re-organisation.

Roberts (1987) has more recently proposed a model (Fig. 2.4) that draws together a wider range of factors that might have influenced the selection of a settlement site. This model emphasises that both the immediate characteristics of the site on which building takes place and the more general situation in which that site occurs are important. It also introduces the idea of perception of particular features by members of a group that could be as important as more definable qualities of the site or situation.

The importance of variations in perception in relation to settlement location is very obvious in some parts of the world. For example, in Africa, proximity to water supply is a dominant influence on settlement location in some cases (for example desert oases), whereas in others it is clearly less important and settlements may be two or three kilometres away from the nearest water supply. In parts of the Atlas Mountains the perceived need for a defensive site appears to have been dominant to the extent that water may have to be carried several hundred metres to a hilltop settlement from a neighbouring valley bottom. The apparently low priority given to being near to a water supply in many small African settlements may also reflect the fact that the decisions are made in a largely male-dominated society where it is usually the women who suffer the daily toil of carrying water to the home.

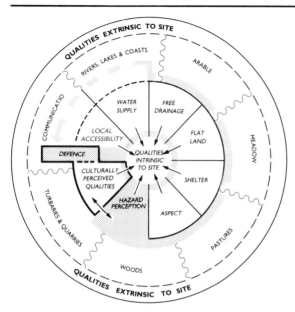

Fig. 2.4 Village site analysis: qualities intrinsic and extrinsic to site. This diagram emphasises the difference between the characteristics of a village site (the land actually occupied by the village) and the features of its more general situation. Thus the inner circle of the diagram is concerned with desirable site characteristics; the outer circle with qualities of the village's general situation (i.e. qualities extrinsic to the site). Roberts emphasises that each village represents a complex balancing of all these factors, with few sites or situations being ideal.

Many of the items mentioned are fairly obvious practical considerations, but two aspects are worth further consideration. First, the emphasis on culturally perceived qualities is important. Defensive aspects may relate to both site and situation and could be a prime consideration, but perhaps less obvious might be aspects relating to a group's perception of a site as being of religious significance (possibly because of earlier usage) or perceptions relating to accessibility to neighbouring groups. Second, the linked issue of hazard perception is also significant. It could relate to fairly obvious practical hazards such as flooding or attack by other groups (hence the link to defence) but might also relate to superstitious fears of many kinds that it is difficult to appreciate today.
Source: Roberts, 1987.

Village morphology

The study of village *form* or *morphology* has raised many issues for geographers and historians, and many traditional ideas have recently begun to be questioned as more documentary and archaeological evidence has become available. It is increasingly clear that many villages have also been subject to short-distance movement, re-alignment, enlargement and/or contraction during their existence and this can greatly complicate attempts to explain their past or present morphology. In very general terms, two basic village forms have often been identified: the *nucleated* village and the *linear* village.

The nucleated village

The nucleated village has three commonly recognised, widely distributed subtypes: the irregular nucleated village, the green village and the regular or grid-iron village.

The *irregular nucleated village* is common in England, in eastern France, Belgium and large parts of western Germany (where it is known as the *Haufendorf*). It is, however, not restricted to Europe and is found, for example, in many parts of Asia, including the North China Plain, north and north-west India and many parts of South-East Asia. In Europe, its irregular shape has usually been attributed to its gradual expansion over a long period of time from an isolated farm or hamlet into a village through the practice of divided land inheritance and the subsequent multiplication of family and farm units.

The second and third types of nucleated village may generally owe their morphology to a later and often planned land settlement, but there are exceptions to this generalisation. The *green village* is most widely distributed along the old Germanic-Slav border in Central Europe (eastern Germany, Poland and Czechoslovakia). Here it is known, depending on its size, as a *Rundweiler* (round hamlet), *Rundling* (small round village) or *Runddorf* (round village). The core of such settlements is a roughly circular green around which the farmsteads are grouped. They probably represent a form associated with medieval German colonisation. In England, too, green villages are thought often to be planned settlements, but their existence alongside villages of other types makes generalisation about origin difficult. What is probably true about all these villages is that the central green formed a stockaded enclosure for animals and humans in troubled times. A more recent use of this village form is found in Israel, where early *moshavim* (smallholders' villages) built in the 1920s adopted a circular layout not unlike the green villages of Eastern Europe. This ensured easy access to village institutions and facilitated water supply for irrigation from a central water tower to the radiating fields. Such layouts are now considered obsolete from the security point of view.

Grid-iron villages are very widely distributed but their origins are diverse. They are found in many parts of Asia and in parts of Eastern Europe, in the latter case being associated with planned settlements along the middle and lower Danube by the government of the Austro-Hungarian Empire as a means of re-populating war-torn areas. In many parts of the world they are associated with the development of mining activity and have given rise to basically similar forms in places as far apart as South Wales, northern France, Australia and northern Canada. Planned settlements of this kind have also developed in association with other kinds of modern economic activity, notably in many colonial plantation schemes (see Case Study 2).

The linear village

Linear villages (sometimes also called *street villages*) are often associated with the establishment of settlement in marsh and forest, and with planned settlements either in newly colonised areas or as a response to changed economic and social conditions. Perhaps the best documented types of street village are those associated with planned settlement expansion by Germanic peoples into Slav regions in Central and Eastern Europe in medieval times. In forested areas the *Waldhufendorf* (linear forest village) was the planned form most used. Such villages were established along streams (Fig. 2.5a), with each farm's land forming a strip up a hillside, thus including meadowland, arable, rough pasture and forest. The most typical of these Germanic planned villages is the *Strassendorf*, the most regular of the street village types (Fig. 2.5b). A

subtype of the Strassendorf is the *Angerdorf*, sometimes known as the street-green village, differing from the true Strassendorf in that the main street broadens to form a small green (Fig. 2.5c) which often contains the church and duckpond. Typically, the farmsteads in all these planned German villages are of the courtyard type.

Planned, regular street villages were also a feature of medieval England. A study of village development in the Vale of Pickering, North Yorkshire (Allerston, 1970) has shown that the village of Appleton-le-Moors, a street village 'of the strictest regularity', probably originated as a planned settlement. The modern village (Fig. 2.6) still shows unmistakable signs of the regular medieval plan. The village runs almost exactly north–south and the houses face each other across a wide, straight road. There are no side streets. Separating the village from the fields are two back lanes. The similarity between this village and the Germanic street villages (Fig. 2.5b) is unmistakable. Planned street villages of this kind are well represented in rural England, and Taylor (1983) has emphasised the growing evidence of widespread planning of English villages either of this type or around a village green in medieval times. Many such villages in Northumberland, Durham and North Yorkshire appear to have been established in the 11th and 12th centuries, possibly as a result of settlement re-development after Scandinavian coastal raids in 1066 and William the Conqueror's 'harrying of the north' in 1069–70. Elsewhere in England many villages seem to have had their origins at about the same time and evidence suggests that many of these, too, were planned villages, sometimes on new sites, sometimes where previous settlements had existed. Reasons for this development are, as yet, uncertain, but one major factor may have been the re-organisation of agriculture into open-field systems at this time.

Brief reference has already been made to the impact of mining activity on village development. In the 19th century, when public transport was little developed, completely new settlements were established by mining companies, often at the pit-head. Some of these have been demolished within a hundred years of their construction but others have been modernised and now house a more diverse population. Many small mining

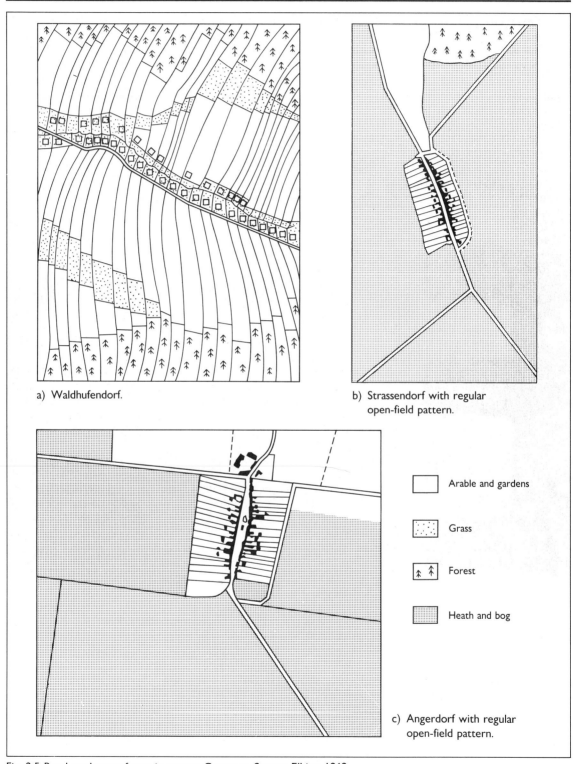

a) Waldhufendorf.

b) Strassendorf with regular
open-field pattern.

Arable and gardens

Grass

Forest

Heath and bog

c) Angerdorf with regular
open-field pattern.

Fig. 2.5 Rural settlement forms in eastern Germany. *Source*: Elkins, 1962.

Fig. 2.6 Appleton-le-Moors, North Yorkshire.
Source: Committee of Aerial Photography, University of Cambridge.

settlements were in the form of street or row villages.

Another variation on the basic linear village form is the fenland village developed on dykes beside drainage canals. In Germanic lands such a village is known as a *Marschhufendorf* (marsh street village) or *Fehnkolonie* (canal village). Such villages, which are also common in the Netherlands and in the English Fenland, have been established from early times right down to the present century.

Linear villages are not restricted to Europe. Settlements of similar form are found in all continents and almost all cultures. In Asia, for example, such settlements may be found on coasts or river banks, alongside dykes, footpaths and roads. Case Study 2 provides a useful illustration of settlement forms in one Asian country, Malaysia, where most settlements might be seen as having morphologies comparable to those of many European villages, though their origins may be very different.

A different classification: rows and agglomerations

Some of the most detailed and interesting recent work on village forms in England has been carried out by Roberts (1987). He suggests a rather different basis for village classification, arguing that there are two basic village shapes: those based upon *rows* (linear) and those based upon *agglomerations*. These two basic shapes can be further subdivided (see Fig. 2.7) in terms of their degree of regularity giving rise potentially to:

a) two types of *row* plan, i.e. regular and irregular; and

b) four types of *agglomeration* plan, i.e. regular grid plans, regular radial plans, irregular grid plans and irregular agglomerated plans.

Each of these categories can then be further subdivided according to the presence or absence of a village green. Figure 2.7a indicates the basic categories of village form dependent on whether this is based on rows or agglomerations and whether these are regular or irregular. Figure 2.7b builds in the further consideration of whether a green is present or not and also provides examples of village plans at selected dates that fit particular categories. Examples are not available for every category but this approach provides an interesting variant from earlier attempts at classification. Roberts points out, however, that there are various difficulties involved in using this classification. One of the most important is the problem of deciding in actual cases on a precise categorisation (for example, when does a 'regular' row become sufficiently 'irregular' to deserve to be classified as the latter, or a strip of grass become wide enough to be called a 'green'?). A second issue relates to the fact that many villages appear to have complex plans that may include both rows and agglomerations and/or have a series of foci. Roberts suggests that such villages might form a separate group known as *composite* or *polyfocal* villages. Examples of such villages are shown in Fig. 2.7c.

Fig. 2.7 Village forms: principles of classification.
Source: B. K. Roberts (1987) *The Making of the English Village*, Longman, London.

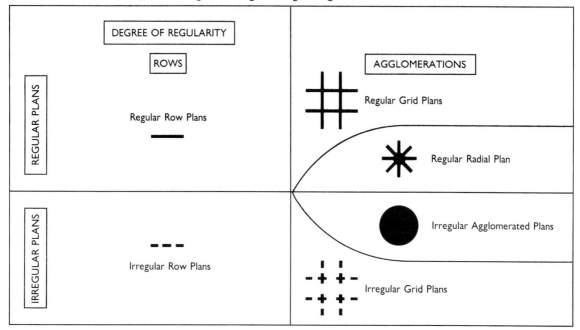

a) Basic subdivision of settlement incorporating rows and agglomerations, with further stage incorporating degree of regularity.

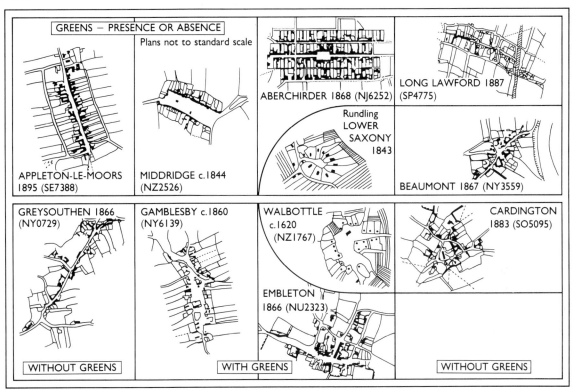

b) Pattern of classification outlined in (a) but also introducing additional element of presence or absence of green.

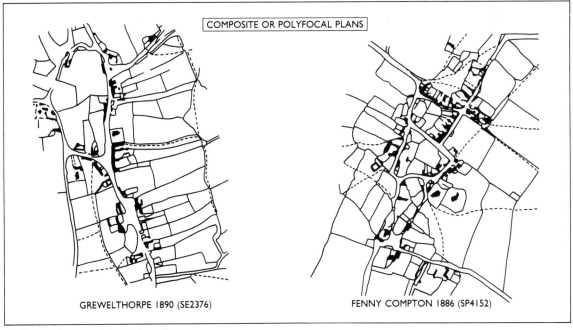

c) Composite or polyfocal plan villages.

The morphology of metropolitan villages

Although villages in many parts of the world retain a basic form that can be seen as being little changed over a long period of time, there is a tendency for villages to develop greater complexity of form as time passes and for the early village morphology to be less apparent. This is particularly true of villages in the most economically developed and urbanised societies where urban influences have had far-reaching effects on rural settlements, most notably in the development of *metropolitan villages*. Also known as dormitory villages, commuter villages, incipient suburbs and suburbanised villages, these settlements have undergone an influx of people of urban origins who, for a variety of reasons, have sought housing in a rural area even though they still work in nearby towns and cities. Some villages also contain substantial numbers of retired people who have only recently moved there. Obviously such in-migrations affect the social geography of rural settlements (an aspect discussed in Chapter 3) and they may also have a significant impact on their morphology.

Figure 2.8 shows the morphological elements of typical metropolitan villages in England. In stage 1 (Fig. 2.8a) a former rural village of nucleated type is being modified by conversion of property (for example schools, chapels, work-shops and barns), by the building of houses on vacant land within the village, and by small additions (accretions) at the edge of the village. In England these features mostly occur in the early stages of suburbanisation. In stage 2, which in England is typical of the period before 1945 and the introduction of strict planning controls, the development of ribbons is common. More recently (stage 3), large, planned additions (adjuncts), in the form of council and, more commonly, private estates, have become the main elements of change. Not all suburbanised villages will necessarily go through all three stages; some will become arrested in stages 1 or 2 (especially if they lie within a green belt), and others may be in the form of village cores submerged by adjuncts without the intervening development of infills, ribbons or accretions. Figure 2.8b provides a model of a metropolitan village plan showing all the features mentioned.

Exercise 2.2

Metropolitan village morphology

a) Select a number of villages in your local area that appear to have some of the characteristics of metropolitan villages (discussed at length in Chapter 3). It is helpful if members of a class can between them examine four or more villages, working in groups of three or four students per village.

b) Obtain base maps on a scale of at least 1:25,000 for all the villages to be surveyed. (It is often a help rather than a handicap if the base maps relate to the villages as they were at an earlier stage of development – say in the early 1950s before most large adjuncts are likely to have developed.)

c) For each village, on the basis of field survey and, if available, documentary evidence:
   i) categorise the different parts of the village on the basis of the elements of village morphology recognised in Hudson's model (Fig. 2.8);
   ii) plot these different elements carefully on your base map to produce a map showing the morphological elements of the village surveyed.

d) All members of the class should have copies of the maps showing the morphological elements of the several villages studied. Then:
   i) discuss the extent to which the villages appear to fit the model proposed by Hudson;
   ii) comment on any divergences from the model revealed by your investigations and suggest reasons for these;
   iii) suggest any modifications to the model that might seem to be appropriate in the light of your investigation.

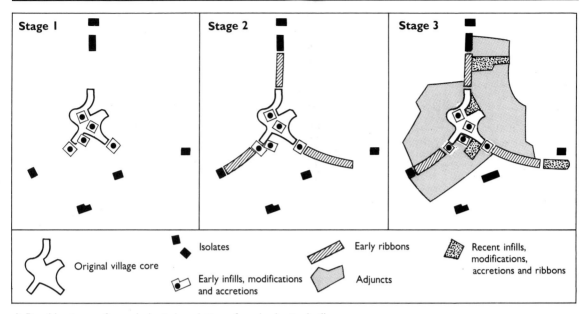

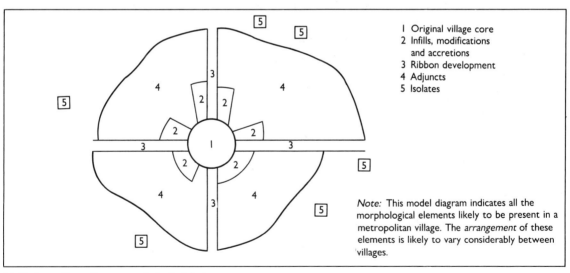

a) Possible stages of morphological evolution of a suburbanised village.

b) Metropolitan village: morphological features.

Fig. 2.8 Morphology of metropolitan villages.
Source: Hudson, 1977.

Settlement form in Peninsular Malaysia

Malaysia provides an example of a developing country where traditional forms of rural settlement still survive, only slightly modified, alongside more recent settlements. In Peninsular Malaysia, rural settlement forms are closely related to the the socio-economic activities of the main indigenous group, the Malays, and the various immigrant groups, mainly Chinese, Indians and Europeans, who moved into the peninsula during colonial times. Most Malay settlements were traditionally in low-lying coastal areas where suitable conditions existed for cultivation of padi-rice – the chief subsistence crop – or where there was good fishing. The typical Malay unit of settlement, the *kampong*, consists of a loose grouping of houses, often strung out in linear form along natural or constructed features but showing some tendency to nucleation in favourable circumstances. Ooi Jin Bee (1976) recognises four main types of Malay settlement related to the economic activities of the occupants:

a) padi settlements;
b) settlements in cash-cropping areas;
c) settlements in areas of mixed cultivation;
d) fishing settlements.

Within padi-growing areas the need to site houses near the fields but above the general level of the periodically flooded padi areas is dominant. Typical sites include river levées,

artificially heightened areas alongside tracks, roads or irrigation ditches, and low mounds within the padis. Many settlements are linear because of the form of such sites but nucleation occurs, for example, at road junctions or on low mounds, especially when the latter are extensive enough to grow a few tree and ground crops (fruits, coconuts, vegetables, spices, etc.) to supplement the padi crop. Figure 2.9a illustrates this kind of settlement.

During the present century, especially in the south and west of the peninsula, many low-lying areas suitable for padi production have been drained and planted with cash crops such as rubber, coconuts and oil-palm. Some are managed in large estates but others are smallholdings and in the latter, factors influencing settlement forms are much the same as in the padi areas, so similar forms of settlement result (Fig. 2.9b). Mixed farming, as described by Ooi Jin Bee, normally involves padi farming in the valley bottoms and tree crops (especially rubber) on the better-drained hill-slopes. In these circumstances, settlements tend to be sited near the junction of padi and tree crops, providing easy access to both types of crop but avoiding the wetter valley-bottom sites. This usually results in uneven linear patterns of settlement. In recent times, these have sometimes been modified by other factors, especially the building of roads that may attract settlement to them.

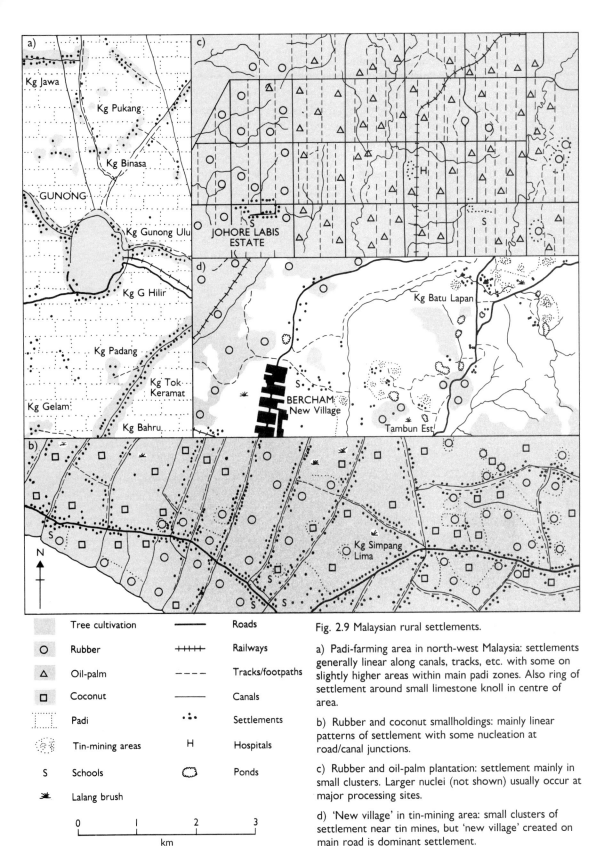

	Tree cultivation		Roads
O	Rubber	+++++	Railways
△	Oil-palm	- - - -	Tracks/footpaths
□	Coconut	———	Canals
⠿	Padi	·.·.	Settlements
⠿	Tin-mining areas	H	Hospitals
S	Schools	⬭	Ponds
✻	Lalang brush		

Fig. 2.9 Malaysian rural settlements.

a) Padi-farming area in north-west Malaysia: settlements generally linear along canals, tracks, etc. with some on slightly higher areas within main padi zones. Also ring of settlement around small limestone knoll in centre of area.

b) Rubber and coconut smallholdings: mainly linear patterns of settlement with some nucleation at road/canal junctions.

c) Rubber and oil-palm plantation: settlement mainly in small clusters. Larger nuclei (not shown) usually occur at major processing sites.

d) 'New village' in tin-mining area: small clusters of settlement near tin mines, but 'new village' created on main road is dominant settlement.

0   1   2   3
km

There are numerous fishing settlements, the main contrasts in form resulting from the varied physical character of the coastline. Mangrove swamps, mud and sand banks along the west coast limit suitable sites, and most fishing villages are on the landward side of the swamps. Some have a linear form along a river bank but others are more nucleated and extend further inland. East coast fishing *kampongs*, sited where long sandy beaches rather than mangrove swamps are the norm, often have a strikingly linear form. Some houses stand just above normal high-water mark and face directly onto the beach. Others may be 50 or 100 metres from the sea among the coconut palms that usually occupy the sandy beach ridges (*permatang*) of earlier shorelines. These *permatang* are sometimes separated by freshwater swamps that may be drained for padi cultivation and so attract further lines of settlement parallel to the coast. In many cases, individual houses may be 30 metres or more apart in a continuous line with no clear break between *kampongs*. Clustering is most usual near river outlets where nucleated villages or small towns have developed (Fig. 2.10). Settlements also extend inland alongside the

Fig. 2.10 House in Beserah, an east coast Malaysian fishing *kampong*. The house is on stilts to lift it above high-water mark, though most Malay houses adopt this style, which allows air to circulate under the floor, restricting damp and having a cooling effect. The house-owner has been making fishing traps used near the outlet of the tidal river nearby. Villagers are involved in both river and sea fishing and many have been given government help in recent years to buy outboard motors to power their boats.

larger rivers such as the Terengganu, where fishing, boat-building and padi *kampongs* are inter-mixed.

The settlement types considered above, though modified by recent developments such as increased commercialisation, introduction of new crop types and road-building, all have their origins in traditional Malay ways of life. Four other types of rural settlement result from very different political and economic interests. These are:

a)   mining settlements;
b)   estate settlements;
c)   'new' villages; and
d)   FELDA villages.

Mining villages mostly developed after 1850, as Chinese migrants exploited alluvial tin deposits in the west of the peninsula, normally using a technique know as gravel pump mining. Europeans became heavily involved after 1912 when tin dredging, requiring greater capital outlay, began. Settlement related to gravel pump mines has tended to consist of loose clusters near the workings (Fig. 2.9d), with some larger nucleations as service centres. Many small settlements were abandoned when mines closed. Where dredging has developed, some mining companies have built strongly nucleated villages, often with a grid-iron pattern of roads, but in other cases labour has been recruited from pre-existing settlements, with no distinctive new development.

Estate settlements provide houses for plantation workers producing rubber and other crops. Many early estate workers were of Indian origin, but Chinese and Malays are also numerous now. Estate settlements may be tightly nucleated around processing, storage and service facilities (Fig. 2.9c), but others are in linear forms similar to settlements in commercial smallholding areas or in loose agglomerations where each house has a small garden area.

In some rural areas, considerable settlement re-organisation occurred between 1948 and 1960 during the so-called 'Emergency', a period of anti-government insurgency. More than 500 *'new' villages* were created during this period, housing over half a million people, mostly of Chinese origin. The settlements were designed to protect inhabitants from anti-government forces (mostly Chinese communists) and to prevent villagers providing food or other items to those forces. Some 'new' villages were adjacent to large urban centres, others were formed by fencing round small, existing rural

market centres, but many were truly 'new' villages in that they were deliberate new constructions, usually tightly nucleated, that replaced more dispersed rural settlement. They were usually adjacent to main roads (Fig. 2.9d) so that government forces could reach them quickly, but many were some distance from their inhabitants' workplaces. Largely because of this, some have been abandoned since 1960 but others remain, many with populations of over 1,000 now officially being urban areas but still usually called 'new villages'.

Since 1956, the *Federal Land Development Authority (FELDA)* has developed commercial agriculture through a series of settlement schemes on previously uncultivated land, usually tropical rainforest. The FELDA schemes, mostly based on growing oil-palm or rubber, housed over 100,000 settler families by the late 1980s, most of whom where Malays. Each settler normally receives a plot of land including a house to be paid for over 15 years or so. Most FELDA settlements contain 400–500 houses arranged in linear patterns along roads that focus on a central service area. However, there have been recent attempts to develop larger service centres to serve a number of smaller FELDA settlements and provide a wider range of employment opportunities, especially as part of the large regional development schemes initiated in the 1970s. Some of these centres may eventually become sizeable towns.

The FELDA settlements illustrate the rapid changes that can occur in rural settlement patterns and the modern involvement of government agencies in such changes. Although government action may help to bring about change, broader socio-economic developments in Malaysia such as urbanisation, industrialisation, improved communications and increasing affluence are also very important. The appearance of many rural settlements has already begun to change (for example through the use of modern building materials such as corrugated metal rather than traditional *atap* thatch for roofing), but much more change is likely to occur in future, as it has in the developed countries.

3

The socio-economic geography of rural settlements

It is extremely difficult to generalise about the socio-economic geography of rural settlements because of the wide variety of economic, political and cultural contexts in which they exist. Although in some parts of the world there is marked continuity of traditional forms of economic and social organisation, in most regions there is change, some of it very rapid. Perhaps the most marked changes have taken place in the most economically advanced and urbanised countries, especially in the regions adjacent to large towns and cities, but urbanisation and economic change have also had far-reaching effects upon rural settlements in less developed countries and in the more remote regions of advanced societies.

Fig. 3.1 Open fields with individually owned strips, Burgenland, eastern Austria.

The changing socio-economic geography of rural settlements in the developed world

The effects of land reforms

Socio-economic changes brought about by the re-organisation of economic activity, especially farming, have been a feature of rural settlements in many parts of the developed world for many centuries, and such changes have taken a variety of forms. An early example, but one that had far-reaching effects on the economic landscape of rural settlements, and which also resulted in some cases in the abandonment of villages and the creation of planned settlements, was the emergence in medieval times in some parts of Europe of the *common field system*. In this system, villagers co-operated in tilling and harvesting two or three large *open fields* and tending large areas of meadow, grazing and woodland, all held in common. The system appears to have arisen as a result of a need to solve the problem of access, and the more efficient working of the large number of tiny and scattered parcels that had resulted from centuries of division of land among sons. In many cases the open fields were never held in common but consisted of a more rational arrangement of intermixed strips in private ownership.

In large parts of Europe, open fields and, more rarely, common fields have survived into the present century (Fig. 3.1). In England both systems began to disappear as early as the 14th century, but it was in the period 1750–1830 that some of the greatest changes took place as a result of a desire by major landowners to maximise production, improve their land and specialise, all made virtually impossible by age-old cropping systems, communal access to land at particular times of the year and the scattering of land across the open fields. This was the period of *parliamentary enclosures*, so called because they took place as a result of local or private acts of parliament. Special commissioners were appointed to each parish and they prepared plans to re-allocate land. Open or common fields disappeared and were replaced by consolidated farms made up of regular fields. In some parishes, parliamentary enclosure was no more than a clearing-up process after centuries of

consolidation and enclosure by private agree-
ment, but in others whole medieval landscapes
disappeared almost overnight.

Land enclosure in the 18th and 19th centuries
was not restricted to England. Denmark and
Sweden, for example, both had similar enclosure
movements. Land reforms, including the
amalgamation of scattered plots into compact
holdings, new road building, new farmstead and
cottage building, drainage and irrigation schemes
and soil erosion controls are still a feature of
rural communities in many parts of Europe.
Fragmented farm structure is still widespread.
Figure 3.2 shows the startling effect of land
consolidation on plot shape and size and on
accessibility in a small area around the village of
Kissonerga in south-west Cyprus.

▬▬ Road	
- - - - Footpath	0 150
—— Plot boundary	metres

Fig. 3.2 Effects of land consolidation in a small area near
the village of Kissonerga, Paphos district, Cyprus.
Source: King, 1980.

Urban influences on employment patterns and land use

In countries where land consolidation has not
taken place or where landholdings are extremely
small, increasing numbers of agriculturalists have
turned to urban areas for additional or
alternative employment, and many urban
dwellers have bought or rented farmsteads, farm
buildings and smallholdings. The first situation
has resulted in a rapid increase in the number of
what are sometimes called *worker-peasants*, and
the second in widespread second-home ownership and hobby farming. These changes have also
occurred in rural areas where small landholdings
are not the rule and where dispersal of plots is
not a major problem, for example in the UK and
the USA. In these two countries well-paid urban
job opportunities on the one hand and large
numbers of affluent urban dwellers wishing to
acquire rural properties on the other, have been
the major factors leading to such changes.

Worker-peasants (from the French
ouvriers-paysans), or part-time farmers, commute
daily to work in nearby towns and yet continue
to work their farms, usually in the mornings
before they set out to work, in the evenings when
they return, and during weekends and holidays.
In the 1960s, one-quarter of all farms in West
Germany were worked by part-time farmers, and
in Poland recent estimates are as high as
one-third. In the Massif Central in France as
many as 25 per cent of farms are worker-peasant
holdings. In the USA in agricultural areas within
commuting distance of towns and cities, it is not
unusual to see clusters of cars parked at road
intersections indicating the existence of car pools
formed by part-time rural workers, usually
part-time farmers. Each man drives his car to the
main highway, parks it, and the group then
travels in one car for the remainder of the long
journey to work.

The existence of part-time farmers represents
one way in which rural communities may gradually
disintegrate. Daily contact with urban areas and
urban residents may lead to dissatisfaction with a
rural lifestyle and a rural location. This may lead
to abandonment of farming and eventually
out-migration from rural areas. Where this
occurs, land may be sold or rented to other
farmers or to urban residents. Whether sold to
urban residents directly or indirectly (by other

farmers acquiring the land along with unwanted farmhouses, farm-buildings or workers' cottages), more and more rural buildings in attractive areas are being used as second homes during winter and summer holidays and at weekends. It has been estimated that at the beginning of the 1970s there were about 3 million second homes in Western Europe, a similar number in the USA, 1 million in Eastern Europe, half a million in Canada and a quarter of a million in Australia. In the most advanced countries, the use of former farm buildings as second homes has gone a stage further. Instead of just buying farmhouses or farm buildings, whole farms have been bought by former urban dwellers who still retain their non-farm employment. Such farms have become known in North America, where they are most widespread, as *hobby farms*. Most hobby farms are characterised by the keeping of a few horses and/or other livestock, but some hobby farmers do cultivate the land. Many lease part of their land to commercial farmers. In the USA as early as 1954 it was estimated that 30 per cent of the nation's farms were either part-time or hobby farms.

The political dimension

Increased efficiency, over-production and resultant changes in government attitudes to financial aid for farmers may also lead to significant economic and social changes. For example, by the beginning of the 1980s the countries of the European Community had become self-sufficient in a wide range of farm products, various food 'mountains' had developed and yet farmers, under the Common Agricultural Policy (CAP), continued to be guaranteed reasonable prices for everything they produced. This precipitated a financial crisis in which intervention costs (subsidies to farmers) were greater than the resources of the CAP. There has, therefore, emerged a need to curb agricultural over-production and to reduce subsidies to farmers and this is likely to have profound effects by the end of this century on rural economies, patterns of rural land use and the structure of rural society in the member states. Rural areas of medium land quality are likely to see the greatest changes with farmers bringing land out of cereals and diversifying their operations both within and outside agriculture. Figure 3.3 identifies four

main areas of potential diversification, some increasingly common, others still relatively rare. As rural areas adjust to the new reality there is likely to be intense competition and possibly oversupply of some services and products. This in turn may lead to accelerated turnover of land and further decline of rural communities.

In Romania, in Eastern Europe, thousands of rural communities were threatened by political intervention for quite different reasons. The country's leader, Nicolae Ceausescu, decreed in March 1988 that the land on which villages stood should be returned to agriculture and the populations concentrated in more efficient units. Critics believe that mistrust of a semi-independent peasantry, fear of the growing influence of the church in rural areas, and a desire to 'Romanianise' ethnic minorities were equally, and possibly more, important factors.

TOURIST AND RECREATION	VALUE-ADDED
Tourism	**By marketing**
Self-catering	Pick your own
Serviced	Home delivered
accommodation	products
Activity holidays	Farm gate sales
Recreation	**By processing**
Farm visitor centre	Meat products – patés,
Farm museum	etc.
Restaurant/tea room	Horticultural products
	to jam
	Farmhouse cider
UNCONVENTIONAL PRODUCTS	Farmhouse cheese
	ANCILLARY RESOURCES
Livestock	
Sheep for milk	
Goats	**Buildings**
Snails	For craft units
	For homes
Crops	For tourist
Borage	accommodation
Evening primrose	
Organic crops	**Woodlands**
	For timber
	For game
	Wetlands
	For lakes
	For game

Fig. 3.3 Areas of potential farm diversification. *Source*: Slee, 1987.

Exercise 3.1

Farm diversification

The map below shows a 120-ha farm located at the coast in eastern England. The holding is predominantly arable but sheep are also kept. There was a good deal of hedge removal in the 1960s and 1970s but since a 'blow-out' on some of the lighter soils in 1986, the owner has become more conscious of the value of shelter belts. In the light of recent changes in the attitude of the European Community towards financial aid for farmers, he has decided to take a proportion of his land out of cereals and diversify his operations.

His son, who will take over the farm when his father retires, has a particular interest in game preservation and is a keen conservationist.

Refer back to Fig. 3.3 and then outline and justify ways in which the farmer and his son could diversify their operations over the next few years in such a way that by the year 2000 the farm economy reflects their concerns and interests and takes maximum advantage of the farm's location and resources.

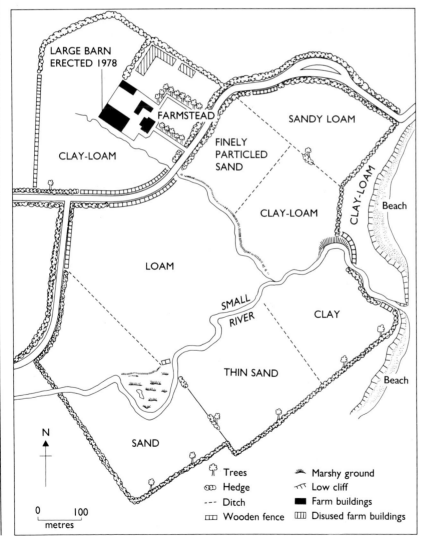

LARGE BARN ERECTED 1978

FARMSTEAD

SANDY LOAM

FINELY PARTICLED SAND

CLAY-LOAM

CLAY-LOAM

Beach

CLAY-LOAM

LOAM

SMALL RIVER

CLAY

THIN SAND

Beach

N

SAND

0   100
metres

🌳	Trees	〰	Marshy ground
⬠	Hedge	⊤⊤	Low cliff
---	Ditch	■	Farm buildings
⊞	Wooden fence	⊞	Disused farm buildings

Source: based on an idea by the late T. W. Randle.

This so-called *rationalisation* or *systematisation* programme was to involve the physical destruction of between 7,000 and 8,000 of the country's 13,000 villages and the forced relocation and re-housing of their inhabitants in around 500 newly built 'agro-industrial complexes' composed of blocks of flats around a civic centre. The process had scarcely begun when Ceausescu and his government were overthrown in a revolution in late 1989. One of the first actions of Romania's new rulers was to abandon this programme.

Village suburbanisation

So far, attention has been focused on the changing socio-economic structures of communities in which the majority of the population are (or were) still dependent totally or in part on primary economic activities, particularly farming. In those rural areas lying within easy commuting distances of major urban areas, farmers and farm workers may form only a tiny minority of the economically active population. Although features already noted, such as second

homes and part-time and hobby farming, may all be present, the most important features of such areas are large metropolitan villages. Such suburbanised villages were, in some cases, created immediately after the opening of the railways in the mid-19th century, but their period of greatest growth, particularly in Western Europe, has been in the last 40 years. The morphology of these settlements has already been described in Chapter 2. They also have a distinctive *social geography*.

A number of writers who have made detailed studies of metropolitan villages have drawn attention to the gradual disappearance in such settlements of the former integrated community structure and its replacement by a dual organisation of two co-existing groups – long-established residents, and newcomers. Figure 3.4 shows, in their starkest form, the differences that may exist between the long-established and migrant populations in a metropolitan village. More recent evidence suggests that these differences are becoming much more muted in many villages. For example, the socio-economic status of newcomers in many settlements has been much more mixed, mainly

Long-established residents	Newcomers
• Born in village or local area.	• Born elsewhere, often in another part of the country.
• Live in council property and tied property.	• Live in owner-occupied property.
• Predominantly in socio-economic groups 9, 10, 11, 15.[*a]	• Predominantly in socio-economic groups 1, 2, 3, 4.[*b]
• Work locally.	• Work in nearby towns and cities.
• Travel to work on foot, by bike, by bus.	• Travel to work by car and train.
• Earnings below the national average.	• Earnings above the national average.
• Average age higher than that of total village population.	• Average age lower than that of total village population.[*c]
• Composite families not uncommon.	• Simple nuclear families.
• Relatives live in village and/or surrounding rural area.	• Relatives unlikely to be found in village or surrounding area.
• Much use made of village shops and community organisations.	• Shopping and recreation trips over wide area, especially to surrounding towns and cities.

[*a] Skilled manual workers, semi-skilled manual workers, unskilled manual workers and agricultural workers respectively. There have always been exceptions to this generalisation; for example, farmers, doctors, parsons and school teachers are examples of long-established village residents who belong to socio-economic groups 1 to 4.

[*b] Various kinds of employers, managers and professional workers.

[*c] Some settlements, especially in coastal areas, contain large numbers of retired newcomers.

Fig. 3.4 Comparison of long-established residents and newcomers to metropolitan villages.

as the result of the in-migration of relatively high-paid manual workers and their families in search of low- and medium-priced residential property. The suburbanisation of manufacturing employment and the consequent attractions of peripheral residential locations also appear to have been major contributory factors. Another trend is the increasing number of long-established residents who commute to work in nearby towns and cities. These commuters are sometimes referred to as *inertia commuters* to distinguish them from the newcomers, or *voluntary commuters*. One of the consequences of the increasing number of inertia commuters, especially if they are car owners, is the decreased use of village shops and amenities, which in some cases has resulted in shop closure and the collapse of village organisations. This issue is returned to in the next chapter.

In spite of the recent disappearance of some differences between long-established residents and newcomers, others remain. In a study of Milton Campsie, a metropolitan village lying about 13km north-east of Glasgow, Pacione (1980) showed that little social contact occurred between the long-established population (85 per cent of whom were council-house tenants) and the newcomers (all of whom were owner-occupiers). Only 7 per cent of the long-established residents and only 5 per cent of the newcomers made social visits with the other group.

The changing socio-economic geography of rural settlements in developing countries

Recent socio-economic changes in developing countries largely originated in the period of European colonial rule. This was in the 19th and 20th centuries in most of Asia and Africa but began much earlier in Latin America, in the 16th century in most countries. The majority of Latin American countries were independent by 1830. Some developing countries were never directly colonised but, as in Thailand, for example, were still considerably affected as a result of commercial contacts with colonial powers. The nature and extent of socio-economic changes vary greatly both within and between developing countries, but certain general patterns of change can be identified.

Before the colonial period, rural socio-economic structures in such countries were usually linked to subsistence production systems. This does not imply that no trading occurred, but most people were principally concerned with producing for their own needs and any trading that did take place was usually on a small scale. Production systems included such widely differing types as hunting and gathering, shifting cultivation, pastoral nomadism and sedentary cultivation with or without irrigation. Inevitably, rural societies related to these economic systems varied considerably but change in such societies tended to be slow and limited in extent, in comparison with that of colonial times and the period after independence.

Factors influencing change in rural communities

Spencer (1977) attempted to summarise the main factors influencing change in rural communities in south and east Asia in the 19th and 20th centuries. His ideas form a useful starting-point for examining socio-economic changes in developing countries, as many of them can be applied to other areas as well as Asia. The following list incorporates many of his suggestions.

1 *The development of improved public health systems*
   Public health improvements, beginning in the 19th century in some areas but usually accelerating considerably after 1950, have lowered mortality rates, lengthened lifespans and so increased population totals. Effects of this have often included a growth in settlement size, shortages of land for cultivation, and consequent tendencies for increased migration from rural to urban areas in search of alternative employment.

2 *Improvements in transport and communications*
   The former near-isolation of many rural communities has often been ended by providing easier physical access to other areas and through the wealth of new ideas that have become accessible via radio, newspapers and even television. Better transport facilities provide opportunities to serve wider markets and to be reached by other producers (see (5)

below). As in developed countries, increased mobility may provide new job opportunities and the chance to experience contact with other people and other areas. This, in turn, may have further influences on village life and society, as Fig. 3.5 shows. Where improved communications lead to the development of tourism, changes may be even more dramatic (see Case Study 3B).

3   *Expansion of education facilities*

Village schools, despite many inadequacies, open the minds of children to ideas that may greatly influence their future. Some ideas conflict with traditional values and attitudes, especially if – as often happens – schools develop on the basis of foreign educational systems or ideas. Education has influenced many youngsters to seek non-traditional forms of employment that are not widely

TEN YEARS AGO when we came to live in the village of Shivangaon in Eastern Maharashtra it really was a village. The fields were surrounded by the fields of other villages, and, although it is only 11 kilometres from the city of Nagpur, part of the road was then unmetalled and buses were few and unpunctual. Since then Nagpur's suburbs have crept nearer, the road has been made up, and the bus now comes hourly. Increasingly more and more of the younger generation go into Nagpur daily to work.

Are basic attitudes in the village changing? Has contact with the city meant improvements in health and education for instance? The question is relevant because although very few of India's 500,000 villages are as near a city as we are, better communications and contacts are lessening isolation everywhere. Bicycles and transistor radios are used all over the countryside.

One striking development in Shivangaon has been a widening gulf between fathers and sons. The older generation still dress in the traditional dhoti, get up at dawn to go out in the fields, and are occupied with the concerns of farmers the world over – the weather, the condition of the crop, and the price they expect to get for it. If they go into Nagpur it is on top of a bullock cart loaded with vegetables, groundnuts or sometimes cotton for sale.

Their sons are increasingly uninterested in farming. They value education and continue their own schooling as long as they can, but only as a means to a job in the city. Since Nagpur has no expanding industry this usually means some kind of government job, if possible clerical. Those who succeed do contribute some of their earnings to the joint family, but an uneasy relationship develops. Tight trousers are not meant for sitting on the floor, so an incongruous chair and table are introduced in the little mud-walled house. After marriage they tend to split off and move into Nagpur. Those who fail to get a job join the rural unemployed, sometimes helping grudgingly in the fields but mostly sitting around under the banyan tree at the bus stop, sometimes enjoying a little mild gambling or drinking.

Either way the young do not contribute much to the re-generation of rural life. Even if a Shivangaon boy should become a doctor, which none has because of the expense and shortage of places in medical colleges, he would certainly wish to work in the city where there is money to be made rather than in his own village.

The idea that education is important for girls has yet to be accepted. Four years' primary education is compulsory for all, but the law cannot be enforced, mainly because there are not enough teachers. Most girls in

Shivangaon start school but drop out after a couple of years. The sad fact is that a girl of eight or nine is an economic asset. She can earn something in the fields, if only by picking up stones, or she can mind the baby while her mother goes out to work.

There are spheres in which ideas have changed. One of these is the position of the former Untouchables. About half of Shivangaon's population of 3,000 were originally Mahars, one of the lowest castes. There is still a segregated cluster of poor houses which was their part of the village, and it is easy to imagine what their lot was. In the 1950s, they came under the influence of Dr Ambedkar, himself an Untouchable who was a formidable protagonist of their cause. Under his leadership they became converts to Buddhism, which he felt was the best way of raising their status, since Buddhism does not recognise caste. They are known as Neo-Buddhists; and although from the religious point of view there is nothing very Buddhist about them, as a social reform it has worked. A Neo-Buddhist friend of ours says there is no discrimination now. Everyone has equal access to wells and roads, a number of Neo-Buddhist houses are interspersed in the 'caste' part of the village, and some of the most successful farmers are Neo-Buddhists. They have even got rid of the dowry system.

Fig. 3.5 Communications and change in an Indian village.
Source: Ghate, 1978.

available in rural areas, so encouraging increased mobility and new ways of life.

4 *Increased mechanisation and electrification*
This factor varies greatly in its impact but in some areas (for example Taiwan and South Korea) has had a major influence both on agricultural technology and domestic lifestyles. In areas affected by the 'green revolution', including much of south and south-east Asia, mechanisation by larger landowners has resulted in a falling demand for labour and attempts by large landowners to acquire even more land and so increase their profits. Such changes can have major socio-economic effects in terms of increased inequalities, greater unemployment and widespread landlessness.

5 *The penetration of many different manufactured goods into rural areas*
The enormous range of manufactured goods now on sale in rural areas includes such disparate items as galvanised metal roofing and other construction materials; 'Western'

Fig. 3.6 A market stall at El Hamma du Djerid, Tunisia. El Hamma is a small, remote oasis settlement in the west of Tunisia, between the salt lakes of Chott El Djerid and Chott El Gharsa. Despite its remoteness, there is clearly a wide range of manufactured goods available that are not produced locally. Consider what local goods have been replaced by these, and how this could have affected the local economy and lifestyles.

types of clothing; plastic buckets and other domestic ware; bicycles and transistor radios (Fig. 3.6). The possession of such items changes rural lifestyles in many ways and the desire to possess them may also influence decisions concerning lifestyles by encouraging individuals to seek a higher income through adopting new techniques or migrating in search of employment.

6 *The influence of government*
Government influences operate in many different ways, usually interacting with many other factors and in some cases being more direct and overt than in others. For example, in China and some other Third World socialist countries, government plans have brought about wholesale social and economic re-organisation linked to land reform programmes. In non-socialist countries, government influences may be less obvious but still very important, ranging from encouraging foreign investment in major development schemes such as cattle-ranching in Brazilian Amazonia, to helping smallholders through developments like the FELDA schemes in Malaysia (see Case Study 2) or trying to induce social change through legislation, as has happened in India in relation to the caste system. Needless to say, not all government plans have the effects intended but they do play a significant part in bringing about change in rural areas.

Values, attitudes and socio-economic change in rural Africa

Underlying many of the factors discussed above that have helped to bring about change in rural parts of developing countries were the different values and attitudes of Europeans from those they colonised. Writers such as Mabogunje (1980) have emphasised the drastic effects of colonial contacts with many traditional African societies stemming from such differences. European commercial, capitalist attitudes to agriculture, in particular, contrasted strongly with traditional views that focused mainly on survival at subsistence level rather than production for profit. Additionally, the common African view of land as belonging to the whole community and being held in trust for future generations was often replaced by systems in which both land and labour could be bought and sold, with land being owned by individuals over whom traditional society no longer exercised effective controls that protected the rights or needs of others in the community.

Africans often became involved in commercial agriculture to pay taxes imposed by the colonial government, either by working as labourers (in some cases on land taken over by Europeans) or by producing crops for sale. Values and attitudes began to change and the profit motive became significant. Ambitious farmers wanted more land to increase their profits and others, in times of need or difficulty, were prepared to sell their land. Thus a landless class emerged and migration in search of employment increased. Growing commercialisation often coincided with population expansion, mainly resulting from falling mortality rates. This put additional pressure on many societies. In areas of dense agricultural settlement such as the Kenya Highlands or the Ibo areas of Nigeria, almost all potentially cultivable land was occupied by the early 20th century. As population increased, holdings became fragmented as land was divided between a farmer's children after his death. The smaller, fragmented holdings might not support a family, giving rise to debt problems or, in some cases, the sale of land. Frequently, menfolk have migrated in search of work, leaving the farmland to be tended by women and children. With families separated for much of the time, traditional social life has been disrupted.

Moreover, even the joint income from a migrant's employment and the farm plot may be very limited and in such situations rural poverty is still widespread.

In later colonial times and since independence, many attempts have been made at land reform, involving approaches such as farm consolidation whereby landholdings have been re-organised to reduce fragmentation (Fig. 3.7), or re-settlement schemes such as that following the departure of European farmers from Kenya about the time of independence. Continuing population growth places new pressures for fragmentation on smallholdings, especially in areas where commercial plantations still take up much of the land. Near to large cities, daily commuting from rural areas is an increasing feature but, while some commuters are relatively wealthy, most are not. Many are trying to supplement the scanty income derived from their small plot of land and may find only casual or poorly-paid work in the city. There is, as yet, only limited evidence in most African rural areas of the kind of affluence associated with many suburbanised villages in developed countries.

Some aspects of change in rural Latin America

Although Latin America has a colonial history very different from that of Asia or Africa, many similar rural situations exist today. The colonisation of the continent by Spain and Portugal in the early 16th century saw the removal from power of pre-colonial elite groups and their replacement by a European elite. Settlement remained focused largely in previously favoured areas but population decline was probably widespread, mainly as a result of the introduction of diseases to which the indigenous population had little resistance. Population decline was probably one factor influencing the decision to import slaves from West Africa to work, for example, in the plantations of north-east Brazil. The power of European overlords led to considerable social and economic change during colonial times, ranging from the spread of Roman Catholicism to the take-over of control of much of the land. By the time of independence (mainly in the early 19th century), the *latifundio-minifundio* system of landholdings was widespread. This is character-

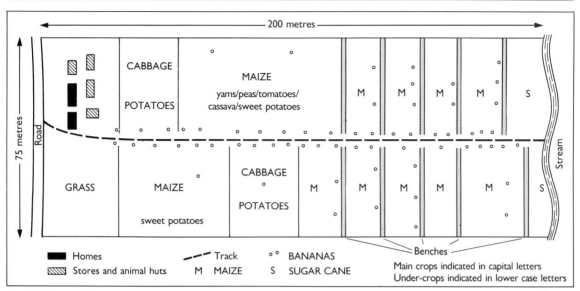

Fig. 3.7 A typical farmholding (*shamba*) just north of Nairobi, Kenya. This farm resulted from land consolidation in 1962. Like many others in the area, it slopes quite steeply from the ridgetop road down to the stream. Two families lived on the farm in the early 1980s – the owner, his wife and six children, and the owner's brother, his wife and three children. The owner had a regular job as a van-driver in Nairobi, to which he commuted daily. His brother found occasional work as a labourer. Most of the work on the *shamba* was done by the two wives, who also kept over 100 hens and sold the eggs in Nairobi. The *shamba* produced most of the food for the two families and some was sold if this was thought advantageous. A crop of beans was usually grown after the maize had been harvested, and two cows were kept for milk.
Source: based on survey work by E.M. Fyfe, W.F and P.E. Hornby.

ised by a situation in which landholdings are either very large (*latifundios*) or so small that it is difficult to derive an adequate living from them (*minifundios*).

Since independence there have been many changes, including the settlement of areas not previously farmed in, for example, Argentina, western Colombia and southern Brazil, that have given rise to many small- or medium-scale family farms; the large-scale land reforms that followed the revolutions in countries such as Mexico and Bolivia; and the recent large-scale cattle-ranching developments in Amazonia. Despite such changes, the *latifundio-minifundio* system persists in many areas with large estates, known by such names as *haciendas* and *estancias*,

occupying much of the land, while in many areas over 60 per cent of the rural population are landless or own too little land to support them adequately. In many areas, rural–urban migration began earlier than in most of Asia and Africa, and large numbers have permanently left the rural areas.

Odell and Preston (1978) emphasised the contrast between 'traditional' and 'modern' forms of social and economic organisation in rural Latin America. Features of more 'traditional' societies include social organisation based on the importance of both the family and the community, of which the family is an integral part; old-established agricultural techniques and communal land-tenure systems; limited trade with other communities and few cash transactions; and strong resistance to change. 'Modern' rural societies have more social and economic contacts with other groups, commercialisation is more common and innovation more easily accepted, while the family is seen as a much more significant social and economic unit than the community. The degree of modernisation of a society largely reflects physical isolation from urban areas but may be influenced by other factors also, an important aspect apparently being land quality, with more traditional societies often occurring in zones of low land capability. Even in the most remote areas, however, change is taking place and, as in Asia and Africa, seems likely to accelerate.

Exercise 3.2

Infrastructural change and land reform in the Kenya Highlands

The two maps show a village and nearby land in the Kenya Highlands (a) in 1950 and (b) in 1990. Using the maps, other information in this chapter concerning rural change in Kenya, and any other sources available to you:

a) Describe the main features of the area shown in 1950, explaining (where appropriate) how the features you describe are likely to have developed in the period prior to 1950.

b) Outline the changes that have taken place in the area by 1990. Suggest reasons for the changes you identify and comment on any additional changes – not apparent from the map – that are likely to have occurred in this area between 1950 and 1990.

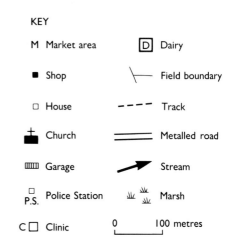

KEY

M Market area

■ Shop

□ House

✚ Church

▥ Garage

□
P.S. Police Station

C□ Clinic

D Dairy

⊢ Field boundary

- - - - Track

═══ Metalled road

➤ Stream

⸜⸝ Marsh

0   100 metres

The dotted areas indicate one individual's landholding at each stage of development.

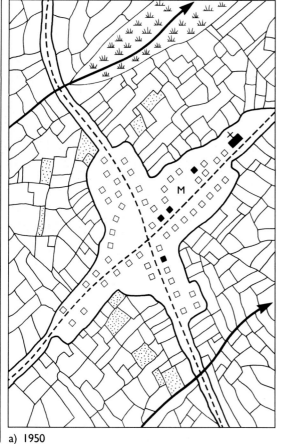

a) 1950

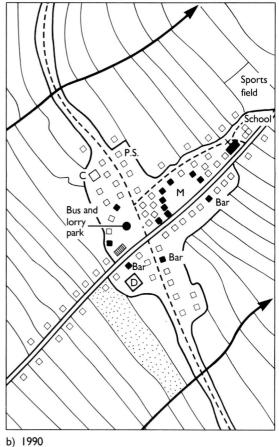

b) 1990

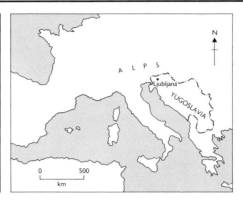

CASE STUDY 3A

Socio-economic changes in rural communities in the alpine regions of Europe

One of the most stereotyped images of rural life in Western and Central Europe is that associated with the pastoral communities of the mountain regions of France, Spain, Switzerland, Austria, Italy, Yugoslavia and Norway. There, so the stereotype has it, *transhumance* – the seasonal movement of animals from one climatic and vegetation zone to another – dominates economic and social activity. The popular image is of small close-knit communities, entirely dependent upon farming, inhabiting valley-floor and valley-side villages, cultivating the surrounding land for grass and other fodder crops, moving their dairy herds to mountain pastures – the *alps* of Austria and Switzerland and the *saeters* of Norway – and returning them to their winter quarters before the first snows (Fig. 3.8).

Transhumance has in fact been in long decline, although it continues to play a significant role in some mountain regions. It has all but disappeared in the Pyrenees, but still remains important in the high alpine areas. In the early 1980s, for example, it was estimated that half a million sheep were still involved in transhumant movements in France. Reasons for its decline, which has had important impacts on the social and economic geography of the affected districts and communities, are complex. The intensification and modernisation of agriculture, including the expansion of drainage and irrigation schemes and

Fig. 3.8 The traditional landscape of hay meadows (foreground) and summer pastures and woodlands (background) in the Austrian Alps.

a trend towards a concentration on fruit and vegetable production and viticulture, have reduced the availability of lowland pastures. Afforestation programmes have reduced the size of summer pastures and made access to them more difficult. Over-production of dairy products and changing government attitudes towards farm subsidies have also weakened adherence to the practice. In addition, the counter-attractions of better paid employment in nearby or more easily reached towns and in the expanding tourist industry have contributed to its decline. The search for second homes by urban residents has also tempted many farmers to sell or rent their underused mountain chalets which are a characteristic feature of the summer pastures.

The extent to which some of these factors have affected a particular rural community may be illustrated by reference to Srednja Vas, a commune in the alpine region of Slovenia in Yugoslavia (Fig. 3.9) which was the subject of a field-based investigation at the end of the 1960s (Thomas and Vojvoda, 1973). Before the Second World War this commune was a traditional alpine community in which transhumance was a major feature of the rural economy. It consisted of a nucleated village situated on a valley floor at about 600 metres, surrounded by an open field system composed of many strips of intermixed ownership; to the north of the village and its fields, the commune extended up predominantly wooded mountain slopes which contained extensive mountain pastures. On these transhumant pastures were scattered log huts which functioned both as temporary houses for cowherds and shepherds and as butter and cheese dairies. The self-contained pastoralist community began to disintegrate during and immediately after the Second World War as a result of wartime loss of life which left an ageing population, subsequent out-migration, and economic modernisation programmes put in train by the post-war socialist government.

By the late 1960s, although outwardly much as it was in the 1930s, Srednja Vas had undergone many important changes and was in many respects suburbanised. Although farming was still the major, or a contributory, source of income for almost half of the community, transhumance had greatly decreased in scale and structure. Traditionally, all the commune's livestock was moved onto the lowest mountain pasture in early May following the melting of the winter

Fig. 3.9 Location of Srednja Vas commune in Slovenia, Yugoslavia.

snows, and then moved upwards through the summer and down again in the autumn in accordance with customary religious festivals, finally reaching the valley floor again at Martinmas (11 November). By 1967 the lower pastures of Naseh and Zajamniki and the highest of Konjščica (Fig. 3.10) were used by less than a quarter of the total number of milk cows in the commune. The reduced number of cattle and sheep meant that the two middle pastures of Praprotnica and Uskovnica were quite adequate for most of the commune's needs and in some places the underused or disused pastures on steep slopes were reverting to scrub. Additionally, most of the dairy farmers, who formerly would have accompanied their animals to the mountain pastures or entrusted them to another member of the family, were using one paid cowherd to take a mixed herd to the pastures on their behalf. This, together with the establishment of a modern dairy in the village, meant that the upland dairyhouses rapidly fell into disuse. However, their usefulness was quickly prolonged through their purchase or lease by townspeople

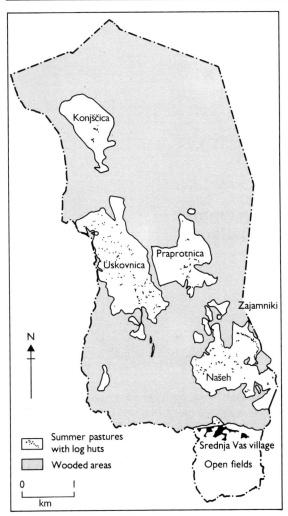

Fig. 3.10 Settlement and land use in Srednja Vas.
Source: Thomas and Vojvoda, 1973.

for use as weekend cottages. Increasing numbers of farmhouses had also begun to offer accommodation to overnight visitors, a substantial proportion of them foreign tourists wishing to walk and mountaineer in the district. Increased higher education opportunities and improved road communications had also made significant impacts on the way of life. Young members of the Srednja Vas community seeking higher qualifications were forced to move out of the area, mainly to Ljubljana 65 km away, and on graduation most had not been able to find appropriate local employment. Thomas and Vojvoda found that 45 members of the 71 families in the commune had left in the mid-1960s. Others, seeking non-agricultural work, had become commuters. In 1967, 54 adults – nearly half of the total employed – travelled to work daily outside the commune. Many were worker-peasants who lived on small farms of about 2 ha producing small amounts of milk and fruit, and travelled to jobs in textile and timber factories in the surrounding district.

The changes outlined above are fairly typical of those experienced in alpine regions throughout Europe in the last 40 years. The intensity of change has varied from region to region and from country to country but everywhere change is pervasive. The combined influences of urban populations and interests, and domestic and international tourism, are likely to make even greater inroads into these once-remote regions by the end of the century.

CASE STUDY 3B

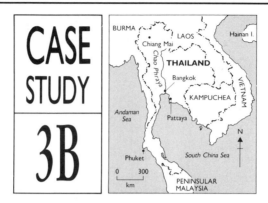

Tourism and socio-economic change in rural Thailand

Dramatic improvements in the speed and carrying capacity of aircraft in the 1960s and the development of package holidays utilising these gave rise to rapid increases in long-distance tourism. Thailand is one country greatly affected by this with annual international tourism arrivals increasing from 225,000 in 1965 to approximately 4 million in the late 1980s. Tourism is now Thailand's leading foreign currency earner (at over £1 billion per annum) and the industry directly employs nearly half a million people, with many more indirectly involved. Although Bangkok, the capital city, is the main tourist magnet, tourism has also had a significant impact on several smaller settlements and adjacent rural areas, and this brief study focuses on two of these.

Pattaya is today the biggest and best known of Thailand's beach resorts. Situated 150 km south-east of Bangkok it underwent early development as a resort when affluent Bangkok residents 'discovered' the then sleepy fishing village with its nearby beach area in the 1950s and began to set up second homes there. Road links were poor so Pattaya was both isolated and peaceful but this situated changed dramatically in the 1960s when American military bases were established nearby and Pattaya became a 'rest and recreation' centre for US troops involved in the Vietnam War. A new road from Bangkok

improved communications and the extensive development of hotels, night clubs, bars and massage parlours rapidly changed the face of Pattaya. Prostitution became rife as girls moved in to work in the bars and massage parlours, many originating from poor rural areas in north-east Thailand where young women were often 'sold' to agents on the promise of good jobs in the south by parents struggling to make a living from agriculture in difficult circumstances. Other rural dwellers moved into the wide range of jobs created by tourism which, though rarely well paid, often offered better prospects than a lifetime in traditional agriculture. The American withdrawal from the Vietnam War in the 1970s resulted initially in empty hotels, unemployment and falling incomes for many people in Pattaya. Since then, however, the Tourism Authority of Thailand and the business community have worked hard to advertise Pattaya's attractions, develop new facilities and improve the resort's image. 'Blessed with miles of white sandy beaches and crystal clear waters', as one brochure has it, Pattaya attracts many people to enjoy its sun, sea and sand and related watersports and other facilities, offering accommodation in about 100 hotels and guest houses ranging from the very highest quality to more modest establishments. However, Pattaya also has about 100 night clubs, bars and massage

Fig. 3.11 Pattaya 'village': the section of the resort noted for its night life with many clubs, bars, massage parlours and similar forms of entertainment. This area contrasts sharply with the quieter image of some other parts of Pattaya.

parlours, and many visitors still look for holidays in keeping with the image developed by the resort during the Vietnam War (Fig. 3.11).

The impact of resort development on local people has been considerable. Many of those previously involved in fishing or farming now find employment in some aspect of tourism whether in hotels, tourist shops and related activities or in informal activities (see Chapter 8) such as trying to sell cotton blouses or provide manicures or massage to tourists on the beach. Results of this include a marked increase in commercialisation of the local economy, the penetration of the economy by many foreign goods, and the beginning of a breakdown in traditional ways of life as values and attitudes change with increased affluence for some but greater inequalities in society as a whole. Some individuals encounter

severe social problems when, for example, younger members of a family refuse to accept traditional patterns of behaviour. Those involved in prostitution may find it impossible to return to their home, family or village because of their 'loss of face'. They are also, of course, at risk in terms of venereal diseases, with Aids a growing problem in recent years.

Chiang Mai, the second city of Thailand, has been the centre of a very different kind of tourism. Sited some 700 km north of Bangkok but only an hour's flying time away, it has become the base for tourists journeying on foot or by road into nearby rural areas to visit hill tribes. Over 320,000 tourists visited Chiang Mai in 1987 (approximately twice the city's total population), and the number of visitors has led to concern about their impact on hill tribes. In some villages, trekkers are present almost every night, with life becoming very cash-oriented, for example with charges demanded for taking photographs, traditional arts and handicrafts modified to meet tourist demands, and tourists paying to watch local dances. Traditional ways of life are gradually being replaced by aspects of Western culture, local social structures are being destroyed, and there are reported increases in crime. On the other hand, money earned in this way provides better opportunities for education for some villagers and brings about other improvements in living standards. It has been suggested that without tourism there would have been more rural–urban migration and some villages might have felt it necessary to increase opium production to earn extra income. To what extent tourism is merely accelerating an inevitable process of modernisation it is difficult to say, but with an estimated £60 million injection of tourist spending in the Chiang Mai region in 1987 alone, clearly some change is inevitable.

As tourism develops further in Thailand, where several other beach resorts are expanding rapidly, and in other Third World countries, it seems inevitable that it will have a considerable impact not just on the national economy but also on the lives of many people who live in rural areas where such development occurs. Very careful planning will be necessary if tourism is to serve the needs of both governments and local people.

4

Rural settlement planning

From comments made in earlier chapters, it is clear that rural settlement forms and patterns have undergone many changes through time. Similarly, the socio-economic geography of rural settlements has changed in times past and continues to do so today. Many changes have occurred at an informal level as individuals or groups have responded to particular problems or possibilities. Other changes have been the result of deliberate planning, especially in recent years.

Planning issues in pressured rural areas in the UK

In many industrialised countries, one of the major results of industrial growth and agricultural modernisation has been a movement of people from rural settlements to urban industrial areas as employment opportunities have increased in urban centres and declined in rural areas. This trend was apparent in many parts of rural Britain by the mid-19th century or even earlier and has occurred at different times in other industrialised countries. At a later stage, however, while employment has remained largely in urban centres, there has been a marked tendency for more people to live in smaller settlements outside the urban centres and to commute daily to work. The growth of commuter or metropolitan villages has been discussed in earlier chapters. The rapid expansion of urban influences into rural areas of Britain, though apparent as early as the 1920s, accelerated after the Second World War and was seen by Clout (1972) as 'possibly the greatest social upheaval since the Industrial Revolution'. The most obvious effect of this was

the rapid growth of population in many rural villages and market centres, although rural settlements remote from urban areas often continued to decline. In the UK contrasting situations of settlements strongly affected by urban influences and those beyond the reach of many of these influences, particularly those where few or no commuters lived, led to the categorisation by Cloke (1979) of rural areas as either 'pressured' or 'remote'.

In the former group, such features as the improved provision of basic services such as water, gas and electricity, the availability of cheaper housing, and more attractive surroundings than in many urban areas, encouraged commuter settlement in a period when travel became much easier, especially as car ownership became more widespread. Similar attractions persuaded many people to retire to 'a home in the country'. The degree of pressure exerted on particular 'pressured' rural areas inevitably varies. Some settlements, perceived as more attractive, more accessible or possibly just more fashionable, attract more demands for housing than others. Such demands may partly be met by the development of new estates or individual house construction (see Chapter 2) but may also result in some older property within the rural settlements being converted for use by commuters or other 'newcomers'. This tends to put pressure on traditional rural dwellers by forcing up house prices and increasing competition for dwellings that have previously been occupied by 'locals'. This can obviously create rifts between traditional rural dwellers and newcomers. The construction of small housing estates has resolved some problems in the past but more recently financial constraints have meant that local authority housebuilding is much less common.

There is also a tendency for demographic structures in pressured areas to be ill-balanced. The numbers of middle-aged and elderly residents have tended to increase at the expense of younger families where low-cost housing estates have not been built. By contrast, if extensive estates of this kind do exist, large numbers of young families have tended to move in. In both cases, the range of facilities required to serve the needs of these populations is likely to be different from that provided in the traditional village (for example the need for schools where there are many young families in a village).

Exercise 4.1

Changing village age-structures and their implications

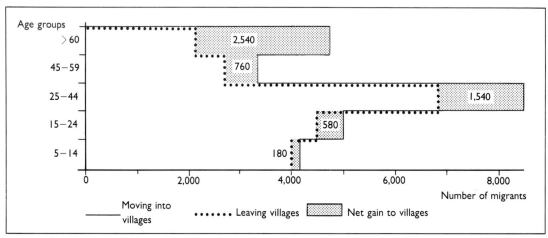

Source: Moseley, 1978.

Study carefully the bar-graph above which shows migration into and out of Norfolk villages during a recent decade.

a) Transfer the data to a table in the form shown below. (There may be slight variations in the values inserted in columns 1 and 2 of the table, but this is not important provided that when subtracted from each other they give the correct value in column 3.)

	Out-migration	In-migration	Net gain from in-migration
>60	2,060	4,600	2,540
45–59			
25–44			
15–24			
5–14			

b) Consider the following statements about rural population changes:
  • Retired couples are moving into villages.
  • Young married couples of local origin are moving out of villages.
  • Affluent, car-owning families in the intermediate age-groups are moving into villages.

i) Does the evidence in your table for the Norfolk villages support these statements?
ii) For the population changes for which you find confirmatory evidence in the table, suggest why they are taking place.
iii) What are the planning implications of these changes?

Planning issues in more remote rural areas in the UK

In more remote rural areas, rather different kinds of problems have emerged. In many such areas the pattern of population decline that had begun in the 19th century continued into the second half of the 20th century, with the 1971 census showing that almost one-third of all rural districts were still losing population (though there is more recent evidence to suggest a re-population of many such areas since then). During the period of declining population, there tended to be population imbalances in many remote areas, usually with a majority of older people remaining in these areas as younger people migrated in search of employment.

The main urban influence on such areas in terms of housing has tended to be in the development of second homes, a phenomenon discussed briefly in the previous chapter. The extent of this type of development and the planning issues it raises in parts of the Yorkshire Dales are discussed in Case Study 4A.

Alongside urban penetration of remoter areas in the form of second-home ownership has been the decline of service provision. Many small schools, for example, have ceased to exist as a result of the decline and ageing of the population. Re-organisation and rationalisation have also affected health service provision in many rural areas and though in some cases small 'cottage hospitals' in market centres help to provide relatively local provision of certain health services, many villages no longer have their own village doctor and rural dwellers may be forced to travel to urban areas for basic medical services and consultation. Mobile clinics have been experimented with in some areas but resolve only some of the difficulties.

Village shops have frequently declined in numbers largely because of the fall in demand but also because of competition from urban supermarkets and other shops that are more accessible to many rural dwellers than in the past because of increasing car ownership. The advent of freezers and out-of-town superstores and hypermarkets with their encouragement to buy in bulk have added to the problems of village shops, which are often left to cater for a decreasing and less affluent group of village dwellers who are unable or unwilling to avail themselves of these relatively distant shopping facilities. Thus both specialist shops, such as chemists or clothing shops, and more general shops, may be forced to close, increasing the pressures on those formerly dependent upon them. These problems are often exacerbated by a decline in public transport services occasioned largely by a combination of increased car ownership, lessening demand for public bus services and the escalating cost of providing such public services. Alternatively, mobile shops may provide access to specialist goods and services not available in smaller settlements (Fig. 4.1).

In a detailed study of post office closure in Norfolk in 1982 it was found that more than 50 post offices had closed down in recent years, mostly in rural areas. By 1980, 150 parishes in Norfolk were without a post office. Although this situation may cause relatively few difficulties for more affluent and more mobile members of rural society, it can be a source of considerable hardship to less affluent, non-car-owning members of rural communities.

Rural depopulation and declining services in the more remote rural areas have often been viewed as part of a 'vicious circle' in which, as population numbers decline, demand for services

Fig. 4.1 Shops and shoppers in Minchinhampton, Gloucestershire. Village grocers have formed co-operatives, such as Spar, to help them compete against large urban-based retailers. For more specialised goods, villagers must visit neighbouring towns or rely on travelling shops, such as the fishmonger shown here.

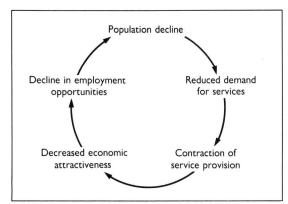

Fig. 4.2 The vicious circle of rural decline.

decreases and provision of such services contracts, further reducing the economic attractiveness of the areas, giving rise to even fewer employment opportunities and so making future population decline more likely (Fig. 4.2). It is important to emphasise, however, that a decline in services has also occurred in many rural areas where the total population has increased.

The planning response in the UK: key settlement policies

Since the Second World War, attempts to influence and control changes in rural settlements in the UK through the mechanism of planning have largely focused on what has become known as *key settlement policy*. This basically involves the concentration of financial inputs into a limited number of 'key' settlements rather than the dispersal of such inputs throughout all the settlements in an area. In more remote areas their main role is to act as *stabilising centres* in a sea of decline, in which services and infrastructure can be sensibly maintained; in pressured areas they are designed as *control centres* to which economic and population overspill can be channelled.

This type of approach has its origins partly in ideas developed by Peake and Morris in the inter-war period. Peake (1922) envisaged an ideal village of 1,200–2,000 inhabitants containing sufficient services to satisfy its own everyday requirements for health, education, recreation, etc. Such villages would be linked to neighbouring towns in which villagers could 'satisfy their

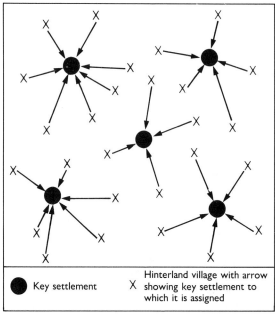

Fig. 4.3 The key settlement concept.

rarer needs'. Something of Peake's philosophy was embodied in the village colleges developed in Cambridgeshire by Henry Morris, Chief Education Officer for the county from 1922 to 1954. These colleges, developed in 20 of the larger villages of Cambridgeshire, serve as centralised secondary schools during the day and as foci for adult education and social activities outside school hours. The ideas and experience of Peake and Morris have been used to justify the 'growth centre' concept as a basis for development of key settlement policies in many areas.

In these terms, a 'growth centre' or 'key settlement' is seen as a rural village in which growth occurs on a sufficient scale to satisfy both the needs of its own residents and those of the population of surrounding settlements in its 'hinterland' for services and facilities (Fig. 4.3). This implies, of course, that hinterland settlements do *not* have the full range of services and facilities needed by their own populations. In actuality, it has also meant that in order to attempt to achieve some kind of balance between a key settlement and its hinterland settlements, specific attempts have frequently been made to restrict growth of housing, services and other economic activities in the hinterland settlements, although these have not always been very systematic or effective.

Key settlement approaches in rural areas in England and Wales have usually been part of a comprehensive approach to town and country planning following the passing of the 1947 Town and Country Planning Act which required local authorities to prepare development plans for their areas. This led to local authorities carrying out detailed surveys of rural population distribution and of services and amenities provided in rural areas, highlighting both deficiencies in provision and variations in such provision within specific areas. It also helped to identify settlements and districts where population growth could be accommodated within existing service and amenity provision (for example where such fundamental provision as piped water supplies and waterborne sewerage systems were adequate to serve the needs of an increased population) and where such provision was already fully used or inadequate to meet current needs. Thus there was a rational basis for planning the lower tiers of county-wide settlement hierarchies. On the basis of such surveys the Lindsey district of Lincolnshire graded service centres into five categories, categories 4 and 5 being the *key rural villages*:

1 Regional centres of 250,000+ population with specialised services such as a university, a theatre and central government offices – e.g. Nottingham (none within Lindsey itself).

2 Provincial centres of 60,000–100,000 population with such services as further education colleges, cinemas and local government offices – e.g. Lincoln, the county town.

3 District centres of 5,000–60,000 population with less specialised services but serving an area with a radius of 10–15 miles – e.g. Gainsborough.

4 Local centres of 1,000–5,000 population. These were small market towns or 'urban villages' with a secondary school and a variety of shops, often providing for shopping, educational and entertainment needs over a radius of 5–8 miles.

5 Rural centres of 300–1,000 population – that is, medium or large villages, self-sufficient in everyday necessities and serving perhaps four to six smaller settlements.

The 1952 development plan for Lindsey, based on these surveys, formed the foundation for policies pursued in the county until 1973. By this date, changes in lifestyle, living standards and population distribution had been considerable and, for example, population growth in rural districts between 1952 and 1972 had been almost three times as high as the 15,000 anticipated for that period in 1952.

Christaller's central place theory and rural settlement planning

Research originally undertaken by Walter Christaller, a German geographer, in the 1930s and subsequently applied in local contexts between the 1940s and the 1960s, has helped to shape thinking on key settlement policy and similar types of rural settlement planning.

Christaller postulated that on an unbounded plain on which population was equally distributed and over which transport was equally easy in all directions, a uniform pattern of service centres (*central places*) would be found. These centres would form a *hierarchy*. At the bottom of the hierarchy would be a large number of low-order centres providing a limited range of goods and services for a restricted local hinterland. The few highest-order central places would provide a wide range of functions and serve extensive hinterlands. Christaller used hexagons to show his theoretical hinterlands, these being the most efficient way of arranging market areas to ensure that every resident is served and that there is no overlap. He devised three different central place networks which he called K-3, K-4 and K-7, the K-value referring to the number of settlements at a given level in a hierarchy served by a central place at the next highest level. Christaller's K-3 method is illustrated in Fig 4.4.

Enshrined in Christaller's central place theory are the twin concepts of threshold of a good and range of a good. The *threshold of a good* is defined as the minimum population required for a good or service to be provided, and the *range of a good* is the maximum distance people are prepared to travel to purchase a good or service. Clearly the notion of a hierarchy, with each place offering a different range of goods and services, and the threshold and range principles to secure

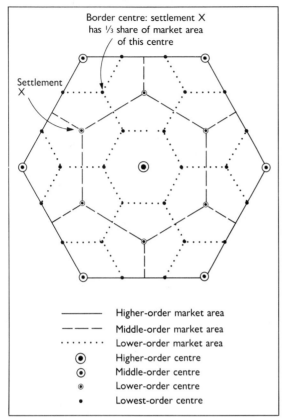

Border centre: settlement X
has ⅓ share of market area
of this centre

Settlement
X

—————— Higher-order market area
— — — Middle-order market area
· · · · · · · Lower-order market area
◉ Higher-order centre
◎ Middle-order centre
⊙ Lower-order centre
• Lowest-order centre

Fig. 4.4 Christaller's K=3 network. The K-value refers to the number of settlements at a given level in the hierarchy served by a central place at the next highest level. In the diagram, settlement X has a third share of the six border, lowest-order, centres, plus the lowest-order part of the service structure of settlement X itself.
Thus we have ⅓ + ⅓ + ⅓ + ⅓ + ⅓ + ⅓ + I = 3.
Source: after Bradford and Kent, 1977.

efficiency and economic viability, can be recognised in the Lindsey categorisation of settlements.

Central place theory in practice

Perhaps the best known of all attempts to apply central place theory to rural settlement planning is that relating to the IJsselmeer reclamation scheme in the Netherlands. This scheme was initially concerned with the reclamation of land for agricultural use, and the level nature of the reclaimed land appeared ideal for the application of central place theory. Figure 4.5 shows how

this evolved in the North East Polder. The construction of dikes began in 1937, the polder had dried out by 1942, and the laying out of farms, roads, villages and towns began in 1945. The polder is more or less circular and so a main road system was devised consisting of two intersecting main roads, one running north–south, which formed a 'short cut' for through traffic from the old land to the north and south of the polder, and another from west to east, connecting the fishing port of Urk to the mainland. The central settlement of Emmeloord, with a proposed population of 10,000, was placed at the intersection of the two main roads. Initially, six smaller service centres, including the mainland village of Kuinre, were planned in a circle along a ring road halfway between the central settlement and the edge of the polder (Fig. 4.5b and c). Following a survey of farming communities on the mainland it was decided that 5km should be the maximum distance from a farm to the nearest village and so the number of subsidiary villages was increased to 12. Each village was designed to have a population of 1,000–2,000, with a surrounding rural catchment of 2,000–3,000 people. The service area of each village would therefore be about 4,000 people and that of Emmeloord 50,000. Figure 4.5d shows the revised plan that was eventually carried out. Since then two further polder schemes have been executed in the IJsselmeer area. It is interesting to note that although these are of similar size to the North East Polder, both have fewer settlements. In Eastern Flevoland (see Fig. 4.5a), originally planned to follow a similar pattern to the North East Polder, one major settlement (Lelystad) and three smaller settlements have been constructed with Lelystad's original target population of 25,000 being increased to 120,000. This reflects such factors as reduced agricultural employment, increased personal mobility since the 1950s, and the decision that Lelystad should serve as an overspill centre for Amsterdam and neighbouring areas. Even more strikingly, in South Flevoland (Fig. 4.5a) only one settlement has been planned, the city of Almere, with a target population of 250,000 by the year 2000. This reflects the growing importance of industry in the Netherlands and the need to relieve development pressures in the main urban areas to the west of IJsselmeer.

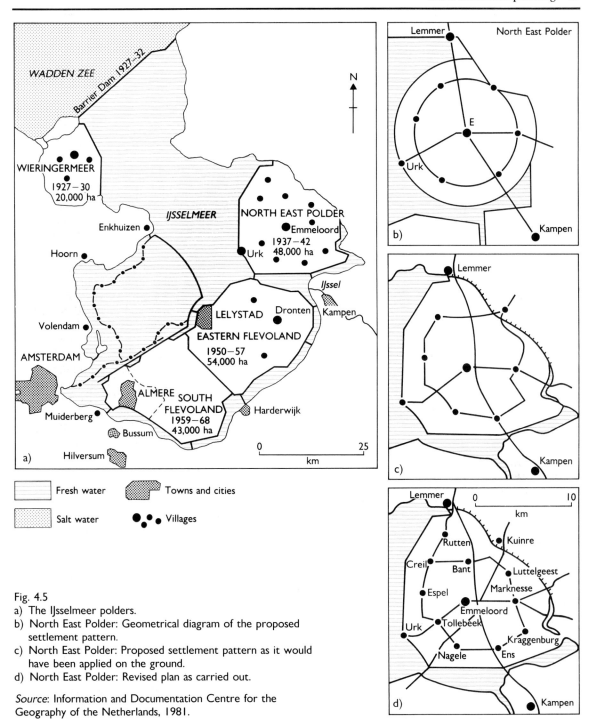

Fig. 4.5
a) The IJsselmeer polders.
b) North East Polder: Geometrical diagram of the proposed settlement pattern.
c) North East Polder: Proposed settlement pattern as it would have been applied on the ground.
d) North East Polder: Revised plan as carried out.

Source: Information and Documentation Centre for the Geography of the Netherlands, 1981.

Clearly, although Christaller's basic assumptions of an unbounded plain on which population is evenly distributed and transport is equally easy in all directions are nearer to being met in the Dutch polders than in most situations, social and economic changes have influenced patterns of settlement. Inevitably, in more complex situations even more flexibility will be necessary if rural settlement planning is to be based on central place theory. Particular problems may arise in developing countries where attempts are made to implement this theory.

Central places in the Gezira

Settlement patterns in which central places have a poor functional relationship with their hinterlands are common in developing countries, especially where larger settlements are primarily geared to an export-oriented commercial economy while the rural population outside such settlements is mainly concerned with subsistence activities. Even where rural communities are involved in commercial production, progress towards an integrated system of central places with a wide range of functions may be limited as Haywood (1985) has shown for the Gezira Scheme in Sudan (Fig. 4.6). This area of 840,000 ha was developed after 1925 by irrigation from the Blue Nile to provide cotton for the British textile industry. New administrative and service functions were initially located in existing settlements, mostly close to the Nile. Later, some new settlements were established in a fairly random pattern as population increased, and later still a series of purely administrative centres was established in an attempt to provide a more rational distribution of administrative functions. At the same time, temporary settlements grew up, often near cotton ginneries, to accommodate mainly migrant labour. Some of these have since developed into permanent settlements with certain service functions.

By 1980, the Gezira had a population of over 2 million living in 1,058 settlements including:

a)   the first-order settlement of Wad Medani with a population of 165,000;
b)   two second-order settlements (Manaqil and Hassa Heisa) of approximately 30,000 people each;

c)   74 third-order settlements with an average population of 8,000; and
d)   almost 1,000 fourth-order settlements, villages with an average population of 1,250, though many were considerably smaller.

Haywood states that about 30 per cent of the villages had a shop, school or health facility and provided a limited service function for other villages, but an examination of retail, commercial, administrative and social service functions suggested that only 19 settlements (Fig. 4.6) performed a significant central place function – a ratio of central places to dependent villages of 1:55. This implies considerable communication problems, but links to and between centres are further restricted by the limited crossing points over the canal system. Moreover, both the railway and the modern regional road follow the line of the river, and electricity supplies and modern water supply systems are also confined to areas near the river, encouraging the development of modern services there rather than more widely within the Gezira.

Finally, services in third-order centres (comprising 16 of the 19 central places) have declined in recent years with an average reduction of 60 per cent of shopping floorspace per centre since the early 1960s. This is linked to such factors as falling living standards for farmers, affecting their purchasing power and persuading many to seek employment in Khartoum or the higher-order centres of the Gezira, while cultivation is left to other family members or wage-labourers; improved mobility via mechanised transport to higher-order centres; and the development of periodic markets that provide a wider range of goods than shops in third-order centres. Thus development to some extent by-passes third-order centres, a balanced hierarchy of central places fails to develop and the perceived inequalities of opportunity and lifestyle between rural and urban centres encourages rural–urban migration. As in much of the developing world, settlement provision in the Gezira raises the issues of whether the real needs of the rural population have been met – or even properly considered – by planning authorities, and whether central place theory is an appropriate tool for planners in Third World countries. A considerable number of attempts to incorporate this and other Western ideas into settlement

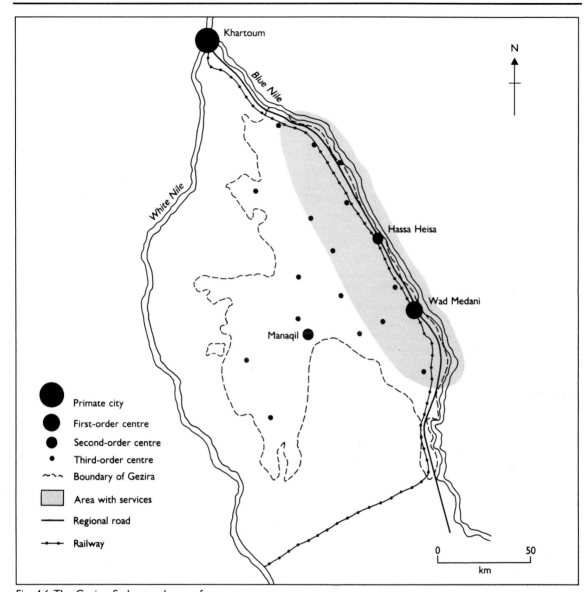

Fig. 4.6 The Gezira, Sudan: settlement features.
Source: Haywood, 1985.

plans has, however, been apparent in Third World countries since about 1950, especially where countries have had a socialist government.

Rural settlement planning in socialist countries in the Third World

Essentially, most rural planning in the Third World has been concerned with overcoming the more obvious rural problems – poverty, inequalities in wealth and the size of landholdings, poor health and education facilities, and the general lack of service provision – and thereby with transforming traditional rural societies into 'modernised' social and economic units. Typically, urban-based planners and politicians have seen rural areas as 'backward' and theories originating in developed world situations – for example central place and functions, growth pole theories and 'trickle-down' effects – have often been applied in very different socio-economic environments from those in which they originated. Planned changes have related to the land which usually forms the basis of the rural economy, to the built environment of rural settlements and to the general lifestyles of rural populations. Clearly these elements are inter-related, but often changes in landholding systems have been given priority, especially where rural changes have followed a socialist revolution, and in many developing countries rural settlement planning *per se* has not been a principal element of planned rural change.

In *China*, for example, the massive land re-organisation following the 1949 revolution that eventually led to the development of communes responsible for all economic activities in their area, for local government, for social welfare and for education, rarely involved settlement planning as a significant feature. Before the death of Mao Zedong in 1976 and the return to a market economy, settlement change in rural areas was generally based on slow, small-scale improvement of existing housing. Since then, the decline of the commune power structure and the availability to many rural people of greater disposable incomes has led to widespread housing improvement and new building (Fig. 4.7), with over 8 million homes being built each year in the early 1980s. Though state plans sometimes helped this process (for example by providing construction materials), in general the building boom was a response to changed circumstances rather than specific rural settlement plans.

By contrast, *Algeria's* agrarian reforms of 1971 included a specific attempt to upgrade the rural settlement system through the establishment of 'new socialist' villages. Despite the creation of many villages by the French during colonial times (1830–1962), approximately two-thirds of Algeria's rural settlement was in the form of isolated homesteads or hamlets in

Fig. 4.7 A village near Zhongshan in southern China in the mid-1980s. Construction activities include both new buildings (note piles of bricks) and the concreting of the village street. This village has benefited from the return to a market economy, with many of the farmers selling vegetables in Zhongshan or the neighbouring Portuguese territory of Macao.

1970, and in much of the country no clear hierarchy of settlements had emerged. The recovery of land from former colonial settlers led to extensive re-organisation of holdings, mostly into large-scale, co-operatively-worked 'autogestion' units that co-existed with the largely unchanged traditional farming sector until the major reforms in 1971. These reforms involved the re-organisation of much of the traditional farming sector into co-operatives. They also initiated the strategy of constructing new socialist villages designed to help overcome serious rural housing shortages caused largely by rapid population growth, to save farmers from long journeys to work on the new co-operative farms and to provide better agricultural and other services than was thought possible if people continued to live in their traditional, widely dispersed homes.

The aim of building 1,000 villages by 1981 was not realised, however, with fewer than 400 being completed or under construction by that date. Problems included weak administration, shortages of materials, higher costs than anticipated, faulty workmanship and criticisms of both the style of houses (based largely on urban housing styles) and the form of villages (especially because families were separated from their livestock). The sensibilities of traditional Muslims were also offended by, for example, locating windows in positions that made it almost impossible for women to have the degree of privacy afforded by traditional housing. Problems of this kind reflect the urban-based approach to planning that is not uncommon in developing countries. Its lack of success is reflected by the move away from providing urban-style housing in new villages in Algeria by the mid- and late 1980s to an emphasis on the improvement of traditional settlements, with the government providing construction materials and a better infrastructure but allowing traditional attitudes to determine the nature of detailed settlement change.

The Algerian experience provides an interesting comparison with 'villagisation' in Tanzania (Case Study 4B), but problems encountered in both these countries have not deterred some other governments. *Ethiopia*, for example, in 1984 began a programme of villagisation in selected areas that was extended the following year into a nationwide plan to move some 39 million people into nucleated villages by 1995. The scheme has similar aims to those in Algeria and Tanzania but has been criticised as being largely designed to give greater political control over rural populations and likely to give rise to ecological problems because of forecasted pressure on water resources, overgrazing and declining soil fertility near larger villages. Whatever the government's motives, the 'top-down' approach (even involving physical force in some areas) must be seen as of doubtful value in the light of experience elsewhere.

Rural settlement planning in a fragile environment

While rural settlement plans in developing countries have often been criticised for not being appropriate to the needs of the rural population, a much wider range of problems is apparent in some cases. Plans to develop the resources of Brazilian Amazonia after the Second World War included the construction of the Trans-Amazon Highway from north-east Brazil to the Peruvian frontier in the early 1970s. This and other highways were designed to serve as foci for settlement, with settlement schemes along the Trans-Amazon Highway alone planned to accommodate 100,000 families, mostly from the drought-ridden north-east, within five years. Planned settlements (*agrovilas* of 48–60 families, *agropoles* of about 300 families and *ruropoles* of about 1,000 families) were sited along the highway as service centres for a farming population of settlers who were allocated 100-ha plots of land (Fig. 4.8).

Problems quickly became apparent. The scheme was hastily planned, and ignored such basic factors as soil conditions and the need for settlers from very different environments to receive technical advice on how to use the land. Settlers often faced the choice of living in an *agrovila* remote from their land, or on their land remote from services. Many lacked the capital needed to develop their land effectively. Almost from the beginning, the number of settlers fell well short of government targets and the early problems led to many plots being abandoned. Later modifications, such as providing larger holdings for pastoral farmers, sometimes helped, but as early as the mid-1970s, planned schemes of this kind were clearly less significant than

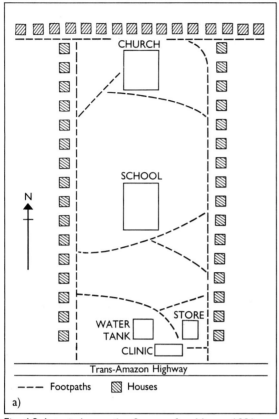

Fig. 4.8 A typical *agrovila*. *Source*: after Moran, 1981.

a) A common type of layout for an *agrovila* settlement with lines of housing round three sides of a central area containing some basic facilities.

b) The general setting of a typical *agrovila* with a series of landholdings (consisting both of land for cultivation and a forest reserve area) laid out alongside the main highway, and side roads linked to this. As the map indicates, some landholdings are a long way from the settlement, creating major problems of accessibility and tempting settlers to build living accommodation on their plot of land. The planned arrangement of landholdings theoretically conserved blocks of forest land, but these have often been destroyed by the settlers.

uncontrolled settlement by small farmers and pastoralists, and large-scale economic projects concerned with timber exploitation, cattle ranching and mining developments. By the mid- and late-1980s worldwide criticism of the impact of such activities on the Amazon forest habitats and the Indian population of the area was beginning to influence government policies and those of international organisations such as the World Bank that had been involved in financing some of the major resource development schemes. Perhaps the threatened eco-disaster in the Amazon Basin may highlight the need for rural planning in general and rural settlement planning in particular to be based on thorough environmental and socio-economic research.

Second homes in the Yorkshire Dales

A study of second homes in part of the Yorkshire Dales National Park (Stacey, 1985) has highlighted a number of important rural planning issues concerning the housing market, community structure and service provision. The study area (Fig. 4.9) covered 14 parishes in Dentdale, Garsdale, Wensleydale and Widdale, a relatively sparsely populated area with the main settlements located on valley floors and sides and separated by high, uninhabited fells. The economy is still dominated by hill farming, though forestry and tourism have recently assumed some importance. Although in the popular mind the area is seen as remote, it is in fact within easy reach of urban populations. The conurbations of Teesside, West Yorkshire, Greater Manchester and Merseyside, with a combined population in excess of 8 million, are within 1½ hours' driving time.

Stacey found that in 1985 there were 199 second homes in the area, nearly 14 per cent of the total housing stock. They were most numerous in the more isolated parts of the area and least numerous in the main settlements. In one parish, second homes accounted for a third of the housing stock, and in two others about one-fifth. There was a tendency for the most recent acquisitions to be in the main villages.

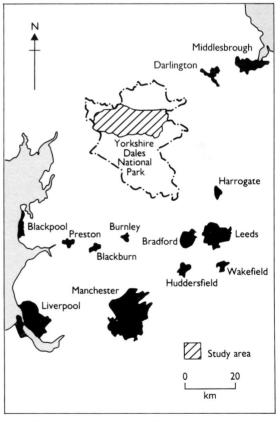

Fig. 4.9 Yorkshire Dales second homes study area.
Source: Stacey, 1985.

A questionnaire survey of about half of the second-home owners revealed that 40 per cent lived in the surrounding conurbations; a further 15 per cent lived in London and the Home Counties. A typical second-home owner was in professional employment, had a high level of educational attainment, was a car owner and so had a high degree of mobility, and was between 30 and 65 years of age, with children aged 5–19. Almost half of the second homes surveyed had been used as accommodation by locals immediately prior to purchase by their present owners; 20 per cent had been purchased from another second-home owner; and the remainder had been converted from barns or previously derelict or unoccupied property. Almost 80 per cent of the properties had two or three bedrooms, suggesting that second-home owners were attracted to the kind of accommodation that might be sought after by less affluent rural dwellers and thus causing potential conflicts between the latter group and second-home owners. Slightly more than half of the

second-home owners questioned said they purchased their main food supplies before travelling to their second home. In the second-home area the milkman, grocer and butcher were used most frequently. Most respondents (72 per cent) said they never used local builders' merchants and hardware stores. Three-quarters said they had not joined any local clubs, societies or organisations.

A survey of 199 members of the local population revealed that 49 per cent considered second homes 'a bad thing'. Only 10 per cent thought they were 'a good thing'. The remaining 41 per cent had mixed feelings or were indifferent to their presence. Most opposition was expressed by farm workers, forestry workers, workers in the building trades and those of retirement age – possibly the groups most likely to be adversely affected by the growth in the number of second homes. Figure 4.10 summarises the main points made by local residents both for and against second homes and emphasises the significant effect that second

	Absolute numbers	%
Improves the standard of housing, and prevents dereliction.	39	19.6
Brings trade to the study area.	21	10.8
If regular attenders, stimulates the local community.	16	8.0
Others (including 'keeps up the population numbers' and 'allows more people to appreciate the countryside').	7	3.5

	Absolute numbers	%
Raises houses prices: problems for young couples.	90	45.2
Causes housing shortages.	24	12.1
Causes community problems.	24	12.1
Bad for local business.	18	9.0
Others (including 'wastes local accommodation', 'owners let their properties deteriorate', and 'destroys the countryside').	12	6.0

Fig. 4.10 Comments made by local residents for and against second homes. *Source*: Stacey, 1985.

	Benefits	Costs
Acquisition	• injection of capital investment. • employment of solicitors and estate agents.	• effect on local house prices. • effect on rented accommodation.
Improvements	• employment in building. • housing stock enlarged and improved. • increased rates revenue.	• depletes stock of cheaper housing. • directs builders away from new building.
Expenditure	• injection of consumer expenditure. • industrial employment creation.	• creates low-paid seasonal employment. • if dwellings were occupied, consumer expenditure would be greater.
Services	• little use of services, but pay rates.	• services withdrawn owing to underuse.
Social consequences	• may revive village links.	• disintegration of village communities. • threat to rural way of life. • polarisation of local residents and incomers.
Recreation	• provides relaxation and enjoyment for a minority.	

Fig. 4.11 The costs and benefits of second homes.
Source: Shucksmith, 1983.

homes are believed to have on house prices. It is interesting to compare these views with the costs and benefits of second homes suggested by Shucksmith (Fig. 4.11).

To sum up, the main problem in the Yorkshire Dales, as in other areas where second homes are widespread, is access to housing for locals. Second-home ownership also has implications for the provision of services as permanent village populations drop below the thresholds necessary to support particular functions. The impact on village and parish organisations may also become severe as some settlements eventually become 'ghost' villages for large parts of the year. In the village of Sedbusk in Wensleydale, for example, half of the 26 houses were second homes.

Faced with the prospect of an inevitable increase in second-home ownership in areas like the Yorkshire Dales, it seems crucial that central government should draw up policies to regulate their numbers if they are not to result in increased out-migration of young households and community disintegration. Among policies proposed but so far rejected by central government is making second-home ownership subject to planning permission so that a residential property becoming a second home for the first time would be considered a change of use. This policy would enable second-home ownership to be channelled into particular areas, for example outside the key settlements, where they might cause least damage to existing communities. This would have the added advantage of gradually concentrating the local population into the main centres where their presence all the year round would guarantee a decent level of services.

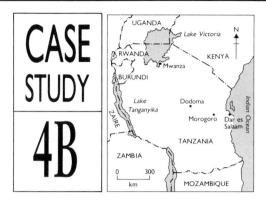

Planned rural settlement change in Tanzania

Few countries have given such prominence to plans for rural settlement change as did Tanzania in the 1960s and 1970s. At the time of independence in 1961 over 90 per cent of Tanzania's population lived in rural areas. Rural farmers generally were hard-pressed to provide anything beyond their own immediate basic needs. Most lived in small, widely-dispersed settlements and so tended to be socially and economically isolated from all except their most immediate neighbours. In such circumstances, concerted efforts to bring about social and economic change seemed unlikely unless initiated outside the local group.

The situation changed little before 1967, though a few small settlement schemes developed with government encouragement, some being based on schemes begun in colonial times. President Nyerere's 'Arusha Declaration' in 1967 ushered in a series of more dramatic changes. At the heart of the socialist policies embodied in the Arusha Declaration was the achievement of 'rural socialism' through a programme of villagisation. Rural development was seen as involving much more than agricultural change, and crucial to the pro-gramme was rural settlement re-organisation based on persuading dispersed rural populations to move into *ujamaa* villages. *Ujamaa* is usually

translated as 'familyhood' in English, and the *ujamaa* villages were designed to bring out all the best attributes of traditional family life in Tanzania, ranging from respect for others to sharing resources available within the family. In addition, it was hoped they would introduce new developments such as improvements in the status and lifestyle of women, better services and infrastructure based on government support – financial and otherwise – for self-help projects within the villages and, significantly, collective agriculture and other 'socialist' enterprises.

It was acknowledged that changes might take some time because Tanzania was a poor country and because the process of villagisation and the adoption of socialist approaches were to be brought about by persuasion rather than by force. Ideally, however, lifestyles would improve and all would share in that improvement. There was no single blueprint for village development or for economic changes within villages, but all *ujamaa* villages should involve some communal economic activities, in some cases perhaps involving most of the production in a newly-established village, in others at first maybe just a small co-operatively-farmed plot growing a commercial crop while people continued to grow their own food crops individually. Massive government propaganda in the late 1960s

	1968	1969	1970	1971	1972	1973	1974	1975	1976
Number of villages	180	809	1,956	4,464	5,556	5,628	5,008	6,944	7,658
Total population in villages ('000s)	56	309	531	1,545	1,981	2,028	2,560	9,140	13,070
Average village size	311	382	271	346	357	360	511	1,316	1,707

Fig. 4.12 Villages and village populations in Tanzania, 1968–76.

resulted, however, in only limited development of *ujamaa* villages or communal enterprises on a voluntary basis. From 1970 onwards government encouragement was backed up by increased inducements, as schools and clinics were usually established first in *ujamaa* villages within any area. In 1971 famine relief was provided primarily to *ujamaa* settlements after widespread drought. By 1972 the number of *ujamaa* villages had increased considerably (Fig. 4.12) but strong resistance to villagisation in some areas and, more widely, to the development of communal activities remained. In general, communal activities appeared to have done little to increase the living standards of villagers or to modernise traditional techniques.

The disappointing progress was implicitly acknowledged in the changed emphasis of rural development programmes from 1973 onwards. The aim of moving rural populations into villages became very much the dominant feature of rural change, with attempts to develop co-operative organisations or modes of production relegated to a much lower priority. The most dramatic changes occurred in 1974–75 and by 1976, approximately two-thirds of Tanzania's total population were living in what were by then known as 'development villages', a result achieved largely by forced re-settlement programmes despite earlier suggestions that Tanzania's rural re-organisation could only be successful if based on voluntary changes by rural communities.

Over a decade later, the effects of villagisation are still clearly apparent in much of Tanzania in the changed settlement patterns, though some areas were affected less than others and dispersed patterns have survived, for example, in the Kilimanjaro region. Changes of other kinds are perhaps less apparent. Communal economic activities have proved largely unsuccessful and there has been a gradual move towards more individual initiatives in the 1980s, with even the nationalised sisal estates being privatised. Reasons for the failure of communal schemes are many, including climatic problems that adversely affected agriculture, difficulties relating to the world economic situation, poor management and, perhaps crucially, the fact that the mass of the rural population were only minimally involved in initial decision-making processes and were never fully convinced that planned changes would be to their benefit. Poverty remains widespread in Tanzania but, on the positive side, inequalities are probably less than they would have been had the trends of the pre-independence period continued. There has also been very considerable progress in improving education and health facilities, with almost universal primary education now established, estimated adult literacy levels approaching 80 per cent and at least a fourfold increase in rural health centres since 1967. Such changes would have been difficult without villagisation but, in other ways, Tanzania's 'top-down' approach to rural settlement planning has failed to achieve much of what the government and President Nyerere hoped for in 1967.

5

Urban morphology

Urban morphology is a rather imprecise term. For some geographers it means only an analysis of a town plan. For others it includes town plan and land use. For yet others it involves the study of townscape, which includes consideration of architectural style, the relief features of the built environment and the building materials employed. We adopt a broad definition here and include the overall shape of the town, details of its layout, its land use zones, and townscape.

It follows from this definition that the morphology of urban areas at the present time will differ markedly from that of cities in the past and that present-day cities will exhibit degrees of difference from one another because of the very varied economic, social and political contexts in which they have developed. Nevertheless, certain recurring characteristics are evident which makes some generalisation possible.

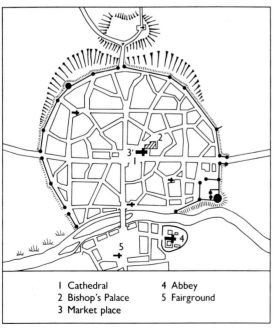

1 Cathedral	4 Abbey
2 Bishop's Palace	5 Fairground
3 Market place	

Fig. 5.1 Generalised map of a typical medieval city in northern France. *Source*: after Fleure, 1920.

Changing morphology of European cities

One of the best-known early attempts to generalise about the morphology of the medieval European city is Professor Fleure's generalised diagram (put forward in 1920) of a typical town in northern France (Fig. 5.1). Many towns and cities in that region date back to Roman times, and their main streets may preserve the plan of a Roman fort, typically sited alongside a river crossing. Once the Christian religion was established and urban life revived, the town gathered round the ecclesiastical focus which was often at the crossing of the former Roman streets. A market place usually developed close by. Beyond this focus lay a maze of streets, particular ones often dominated by a specific craft or trade. Beyond lay the town wall, sometimes with a castle. Variants on this theme of location on an important route (for example at a terminus, a meeting of routes or a water-crossing point), with church and market dominating the town plan, and with both under the protection of a wall or castle, are found throughout Europe, and elements of this general type can even be detected in the earliest towns established in North America.

Such compact and overwhelmingly 'pedestrian' towns began to change in the late 18th century and, more commonly, the 19th century. Figure 5.2 suggests a generalised sequence of development in a British city since about 1800. Although a number of features are specific to British conditions, the general sequence of events and the various morphological elements are common to all European, North American and Australasian towns and cities. In the diagram the relatively small but densely developed urban area in 1800 is surrounded by a fringe belt in which are located a number of urban-oriented land uses which have developed because they have been excluded from the town (for example isolation hospitals, noxious industry) or because they prefer to distance themselves from the urban core (for example the 'country' estates of rich merchants) or because they require certain resources not available in the tightly packed urban area (for example water power sites for certain industries, or farming land in the case of market gardeners and farmers).

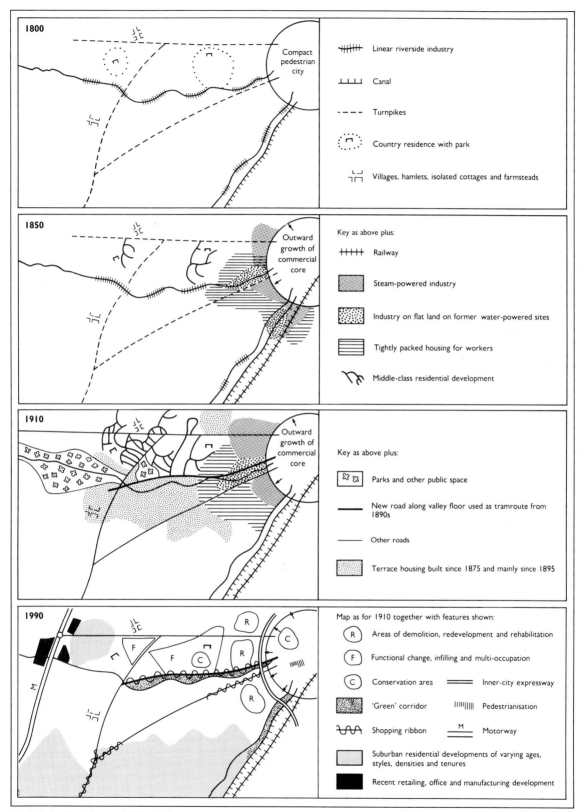

Fig. 5.2 An English city 1800–1990: a generalised sequence of morphological change.

By the mid-19th century important changes were beginning to take place. Industry was now reliant upon steam power and locations near to coal supply depots became important and therefore the beginnings of important industrial zones developed around the old core. In close proximity to the factories, tightly packed residential areas for the workers were erected mainly in the form of brick terraces. At the same time, the middle and upper classes moved to the former fringe belt on the periphery where large villas, often of stone, were springing up. The former old town was now less of a mixture of industry, shops, offices and residences, and was evolving as the commercial heart of the urban area in which specialist shops, offices and financial institutions were beginning to predominate.

By the end of the first decade of the 20th century the zones that were beginning to emerge 60 years earlier were firmly established. Housing and environmental standards had risen, however, as evidenced by the provision of public open spaces and housing that complied with certain minimum building and environmental standards. The rapid outward extension of the city had been facilitated by the development of public transport and this had resulted in the engulfment of a number of farms, hamlets and villages, and in the emergence of a star-shaped city as urban development followed the radial rail and tram routes into the countryside.

Between 1910 and the present day the city, mainly in the form of residential suburbs, has continued to spread outwards, at first mainly in a ribbon form along the main transport routes but later more compactly as green belt legislation (see Chapter 9) prevented further expansion. On the main roads leading from the centre, retailing ribbons extended well into the suburbs, occasionally swelling to form substantial shopping centres.

The more central parts of the city have also undergone dramatic changes. Pedestrianisation of some parts of the central shopping area has taken place and this, together with the inner-city expressway, helps to ease traffic congestion. Another characteristic of the central area by the 1990s is the concentration there of high-rise office and public buildings. In that part of the inner city outside the central commercial core lies a zone of decay, change and improvement. In some parts old workshops and warehouses are giving way to shops and offices as the commercial core expands; in others early terraces have been replaced by high-rise residential developments or new factory units. In some cases housing improvement schemes have given a new lease of life to old residential areas. Some of these have been 'gentrified', as a result of which young middle-class professional households have gradually displaced working-class households. Some of the larger Victorian villas have undergone changes of function and are now offices, or have been converted into bed-sitters.

More dramatically, in visual terms, former industrial premises such as mills and warehouses have been converted to residential use, especially where they overlook water along rivers or canals. Advantage has also often been taken of the decline and abandonment of industrial properties along rivers and canals to 'green' inner-city environments in order to create more pleasant surroundings for inner-city residents and workers and to make such areas more attractive to developers and manufacturers. Such projects have involved cleaning up the rivers and canals, stabilising banks, landscaping, seeding and planting, creating waterside walks, and providing seating and signposting.

Perhaps the most dramatic morphological changes in recent years have taken place on the urban periphery, especially where motorways approach the edge of the urban area. Not only have such areas seen a dramatic expansion of residential development to suit the needs of young home buyers requiring relatively cheap first homes near to good communication networks, they have also provided attractive sites for modern industry, for offices, for warehouses and distribution depots, and for new retail developments. Large superstores and hypermarkets are now commonplace in the urban periphery all over Western Europe, and out-of-town 'regional centres' that rival town-centre shopping areas in their size and range, such as the Metro Centre in Tyne and Wear and the Meadowhall Centre on the edge of Sheffield, look set to become major landmarks in the townscape of the late 1990s.

Townscape analysis

Not surprisingly, few successful attempts have been made to generalise about townscape from the point of view of devising descriptive terms which at one and the same time denote layout, land use, style and age. One of the best known is that of Professor A.E. Smailes who, in 1955, suggested a 'schematic representation of British town structure' which included a number of new terms useful in describing the totality of the townscape. Smailes observed that a laborious building-by-building survey was not necessary, and that in many detailed surveys it was all too easy to end by failing to see the town for its buildings. What he advocated was a 'rapid reconnaissance survey' in the field (including recording from commanding viewpoints) followed by map and aerial photograph analysis.

Smailes' research led him to view the townscape of a British town or city as a series of four imperfect concentric zones. Each zone will be distorted and interrupted by major communication links, by natural features such as rivers and lakes, and by the persistence of enclaves such as commons, university precincts and engulfed villages. Smailes also emphasised that the townscape will be in constant flux with continuous but uneven outward expansion and internal change taking place.

At the centre of the urban area is the *kernel*, the historic core, identified by its commercial function, its street pattern, its individual buildings and the mixture of architectural styles and building materials. Beyond the kernel lie the *integuments*. The *inner integuments* are mainly

Exercise 5.1

Townscape analysis

Make a study of the townscape of a town or city with which you are familiar, as follows:

a) Choose a quadrant (an arc of 90°) stretching from the centre to the urban fringe.

b) On a tracing placed over a suitable base map, say 6 inches to 1 mile, and using a combination of cartographic, photographic and field investigation as appropriate, complete a 'broad brush' townscape map using the adjacent key adapted from Smailes. Do not worry about odd areas not covered by the key.

c) On your map try to delimit by a bold line in each case, the *kernel*, the *inner integuments*, the *outer integuments* and the *urban fringe*.

d) Using Case Study 5A as a model, write a descriptive and explanatory account of the townscape you have mapped.

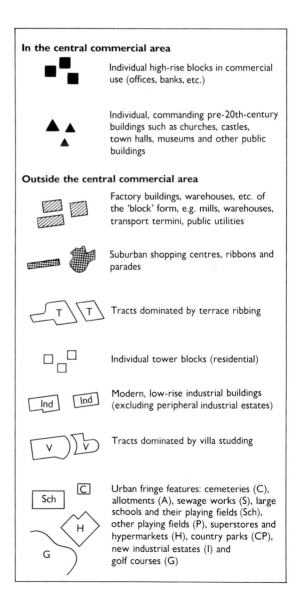

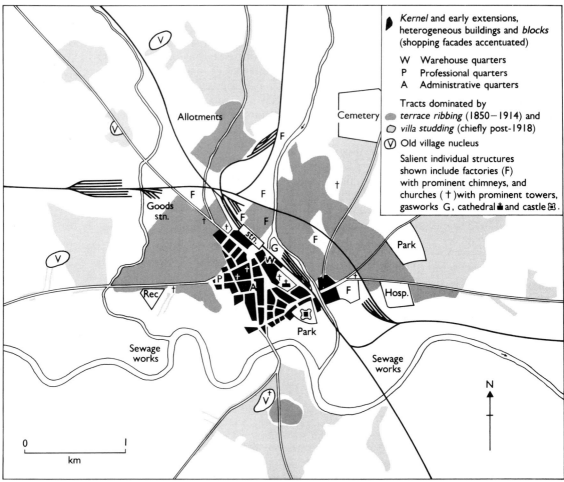

Fig. 5.3 Schematic representation of British town structure, related especially to an old-established county town. *Source*: Smailes, 1964.

of 19th century date and are typically of mixed use with workshops, cramped factories, warehouses, railway land, tightly packed houses and high flats. The *outer integuments* present a less complex picture of more obviously differentiated townscapes dominated by varying tracts of owner-occupied and municipal residential estate layouts. These are separated from industrial estates and commercial ribbons and clusters. The outer integuments merge imperceptibly with the *urban fringe*, Smailes' outermost zone, in which surviving farmhouses and farmland, market gardens and allotments are found amongst residential ribbons and outliers, urban utilities such as cemeteries and sewage works and amenity space.

Smailes associated distinctive townscape 'forms' with the first three of his four zones. In the kernel he drew attention to dominant historical features such as castle keeps and church towers and high blocks, both Victorian and Edwardian, with rugged profiles and irregular cornices, and modern town blocks of concrete and glass. Smailes called these *blocks*. In the inner integuments row after row of two-storey *terrace housing* in formal layouts was in Smailes' view the dominant form, although this monotonous townscape is interrupted by factory chimneys, church spires and the rugged outlines of Victorian schools and chapels. Beyond, in the outer integuments, the terrace house is replaced by the *villa* in the form of detached and

	Growth phase	Functional zone	Relief	Fabric materials
KERNEL	Old town	Enclave(s). Commercial *core* with prongs outside kernel. Ousting of residence.	Architectural dominants, e.g. castle towers, church spires. High buildings: point blocks; rugged profile; irregular street cornice.	Traditional, or imported stone. Concrete, replacing traditional materials.
INTEGUMENTS	Late 18th and early 19th century	Decayed inner zone of mixed use. Workshops, cramped factories, warehouses, high-density residence (slums and high flats); railway space. Professional and administrative quarters.	Low buildings; little relief except churches; terrace housing in formal layouts; some replacement with flat blocks.	Mixed. Brick or stucco and slate.
	Railway age before 1914	Industry and tightly-packed housing mixed.	Terrace-ribbing with factory and neo-Gothic church salients. Gas-holders.	
	Railway and automobile age since 1919	Industry and housing segregated. Villa housing in open, bourgeois suburbs and municipal estates. Spacious factory lay-outs Village enclaves.	Villa-studding. Intermixture of roofs and tree tops. Factory scaling: low buildings with extensive continuous roof surfaces. Power-station chimneys and cooling towers.	Brick, rough cast, and tile. Much foliage. Traditional.
	Urban fringe	Interim development; residential ribbons and outliers; urban utilities, e.g. cemeteries, sewage works; amenity space and surviving farmland, allotments and market gardens.		

Note In Scotland, residence in inner integuments is represented mainly by high tenements, exclusively in stone. Tenements continue as important building forms after 1919, and rough-cast brick buildings only recently modify the stone tradition.

Fig. 5.4 Components and characteristics of British townscapes.
Source: simplified from Smailes, 1964.

semi-detached houses and bungalows in brick and tile set in their own gardens along tree-lined streets.

When multiplied over tracts of the urban area the blocks, terraces and villas produce distinctive textures of relief which Smailes called *block clumping*, *terrace ribbing*, and *villa studding*.

Figure 5.3 was devised by Smailes to illustrate the type of townscape map that can be produced using this approach. It relates especially to an old-established county town. The accompanying table (Fig. 5.4), also adapted from Smailes, gives further details of this method of townscape analysis.

The morphology of 'colonial' cities

Early developments

The economic changes that occurred in Europe from the 18th century onwards and so strongly influenced urban development there and subsequently in other areas such as North America and Australasia, had different impacts in some other parts of the world. Contacts with Africa, Asia and Latin America, some of which had been established earlier, mainly as a result of Spanish and Portuguese colonial expansion, developed rapidly as the potential value of such areas to industrialising nations became apparent. These contacts were instrumental in the growth of cities, especially port cities, and though the cultural variety of the areas concerned has meant that many differences exist between such cities, their present morphologies include some common elements.

It has become usual to refer to such cities as *colonial cities*. This does not refer to their present political situation but to the fact that most of them underwent major expansion during a period of colonisation by a European country and still have many characteristics that relate to that period. The colonial influence was often restrictive in economic terms with the cities serving mainly as administrative and trading centres and with industrial ventures limited to fairly simple processing and craft industries. Much of the trade was often in the hands of non-indigenous groups such as the Chinese or Indians in South-East Asia, the Indians in East Africa and the Jews in North Africa. Such groups often remained separate from both the colonial rulers and the indigenous population, and this is reflected in the morphology of colonial cities at the present time in such features as the 'Chinatowns' of many cities in South-East Asia and the Jewish *mellahs* of many North African cities.

In some cases the colonial administrative and commercial areas and the modern residential areas have been 'grafted' onto an older urban settlement to give a 'dual city', each part of which has radically different features. Many cities in what was formerly British India display this dual character, as do most of the former French colonial cities of north-west Africa. Marrakesh, for example (Fig. 5.5), was founded in the 11th century and developed as a typical Arab city, dominated by the Koutoubia mosque and minaret and with a multitude of narrow, shaded streets flanked by workshops or the backs of houses which face into courtyards. This part of the city, the *medina*, which includes a Jewish quarter, the *mellah*, has remained clearly separated by its surrounding wall and its distinctive morphology from the modern city, initially developed under French rule and formally laid out with wide tree-lined boulevards, French-style cafés and shops and blocks of flats.

In other cases, colonial powers developed planned cities on sites which had previously been unpopulated or occupied by only small numbers of people. Singapore is a classic example of such a city, planned by Sir Stamford Raffles in a form that allocated European, Chinese, Indian and indigenous groups to separate areas and determined morphological patterns that are still apparent to some extent today (see Fig. 5.6).

Planned colonial cities had developed much earlier in Spanish colonial territories in Latin America. From the early 16th century an almost uniform pattern of urban morphology developed in these areas because the 'Laws of the Indies' regulated such items as street pattern (a grid with regular east–west and north–south streets and a central plaza), street width and the location of the church and certain administrative buildings adjacent to the central plaza. The central part of the city was also its economic and administrative core, though industrial and social class decreased with distance from the plaza, a feature common in many pre-industrial cities.

McGee (1967) has recognised, in addition to 'grafted' and 'planned' colonial cities, a third type in South-East Asia. This is the 'indigenous' city which, while never undergoing a period of colonial rule, has nevertheless been influenced by the activities of colonial powers. Thus, for example, he sees Bangkok as a city that has many of the socio-economic and morphological characteristics of colonial cities in South-East Asia, including areas dominated by alien groups and so taking on characteristic morphological features associated with such groups in other colonial cities in that region. Clearly many individual differences exist between colonial cities but there have been several recent attempts to generalise about the morphology of such

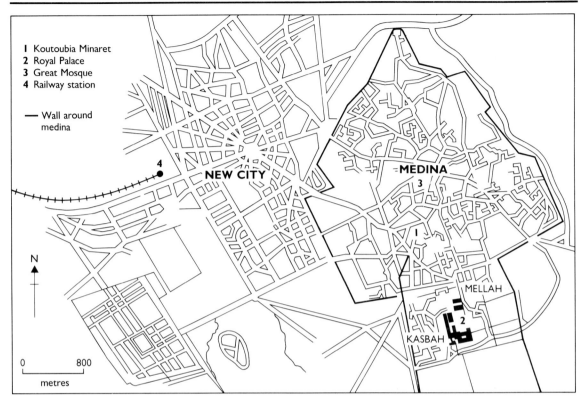

1 Koutoubia Minaret
2 Royal Palace
3 Great Mosque
4 Railway station

— Wall around
   medina

Fig. 5.5 Marrakesh, Morocco.

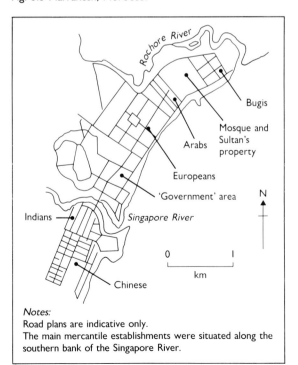

Notes:
Road plans are indicative only.
The main mercantile establishments were situated along the
southern bank of the Singapore River.

Fig. 5.6 Raffles' plan for Singapore City. Singapore was
founded in 1819 and this early plan shows that land
allocated for European housing and the government area
occupied the largest zone of the city, although in 1824
there were fewer than 100 European residents and
more than 3,000 Chinese. Arabs and Bugis (from
Indonesia) were allocated land near the Sultan's
residence in the north, with the Chinese and Indian
communities in the south close to the harbour area on
the Singapore River. Today people of Chinese origin
form the dominant group in all parts of the city, which
has undergone drastic changes in recent years (see Case
Study 9).
Source: after McGee, 1967.

cities. The work of Griffin and Ford (1980) in Latin America and of McGee, already briefly mentioned, in South-East Asia, provide interesting illustrations of this.

More recent changes in Latin America

Griffin and Ford have argued that since the 1930s many large urban settlements in Latin America (e.g. Mexico City and Bogotá) have undergone a rapid transformation from the pattern that had developed in accordance with the Laws of the Indies and remained relatively static for several hundred years. The central areas of such cities have developed a markedly different townscape from that which previously existed, as a result of street widening for modern traffic, the demolition of old buildings and their replacement by high-rise offices, hotels and restaurants, shops and communication terminals, as a modern central business district has evolved (Fig. 5.7). Industries, with their need for urban services such as water and power supplies, also tend to be near the city centre, though in less specialised industrial zones than are common in many developed countries.

Griffin and Ford suggest that this modernisation of the central part of the city has been accompanied by the development of a commercial 'spine' extending from the centre in one direction and surrounded by an elite residential sector (Fig. 5.7) occupied by those who would previously have lived near the central plaza. The spine is basically an extension of the central business district, usually along an arterial routeway, with high-quality shops, restaurants, entertainment centres, light industry, offices and services for the affluent groups who live nearby. The development of the relatively restricted spine/elite sector is perhaps a response to such factors as the limited growth of high-quality services possible in an urban society where few people are wealthy, where conservative loan policies and high interest rates restrict speculative investment, and where the generally poor communications encourage those using high-quality services to live close to the area where they are available.

Outside the spine/elite sector Griffin and Ford recognise a pattern of three concentric zones: a zone of maturity, a zone of *in situ* accretion and a zone of peripheral squatter settlements. This

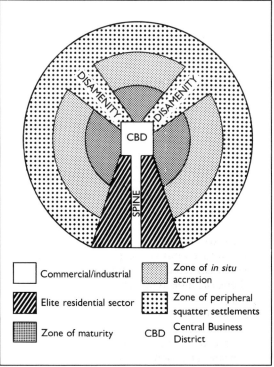

☐	Commercial/industrial	▦	Zone of *in situ* accretion
▨	Elite residential sector	⦂⦂	Zone of peripheral squatter settlements
▦	Zone of maturity	CBD	Central Business District

Fig. 5.7 Generalised model of Latin American city structure.
Source: Griffin and Ford, 1980.

general pattern may be broken by sectors with 'high disamenity' such as valleys liable to flood or areas of steep slopes which may be unimproved or at some stage occupied by squatters. Land use in the three zones is mixed but with only limited commercial activity. The width of zones varies with the outer zone of squatter settlements being widest in cities subject to most rapid in-migration. Boundaries between zones may be unclear in places and gradual change is a feature of the whole urban environment.

The *zone of maturity* usually contains both older housing of traditional style and some more recent residential development. The traditional housing, once occupied largely by those now resident in the elite sector, has filtered down (see Chapter 7) to less affluent urban dwellers. More recent developments may be self-built but are of permanent building materials and have usually been upgraded to quite a good quality through time. This zone has a full range of services including water supplies, sewerage, electricity, paved roads and public transport, and there is normally little open unused space.

The *zone of in situ accretion* is characterised by a wide variety of housing types and quality, some comparable to that in the zone of maturity but much still in process of extension or improvement. Evidence of current constructional activity is widespread. Typically, only the main streets have a good surface; some areas are without electricity, and adequate water supplies and sewerage facilities are not yet available. Some large-scale government housing projects may be in process but the general impression is one of chaos rather than planned development.

The outermost *zone of squatter settlements* tends to be occupied by the most recent in-migrants to the city. It typically has very few services and contains the poorest housing with homes constructed of wood, flattened oil-cans, polythene or, indeed, anything the occupants can manage to scavenge. Water usually has to be carried from communal taps almost permanently 'signposted' by queues of women and children. Streets are unpaved and unlit but some homes may 'pirate' electricity from nearby power lines. Open trenches serve as sewers and waste piles up in spare corners, especially where informal industries develop. As in the other zones, however, the situation is far from static and there is ample evidence of housing being improved and services slowly extended in the older parts of the zone, while new communities develop on its outer margins.

The development of South-East Asian cities

The morphology of large colonial cities in South-East Asia shows both contrasts and similarities with that of Latin American cities. Most South-East Asian cities have developed mainly since the early or mid-19th century, though some existed earlier. Many are ports and most included in their population, in addition to the European colonialists and the indigenous people, a large 'alien' group of migrants from India or China who dominated the commercial activities of the city. Mixing between ethnic groups has been limited, so distinct Westernised and Asian commercial areas have developed, the latter often dominated by shophouses combining residential and commercial functions. Similarly, residential planning in colonial times was often

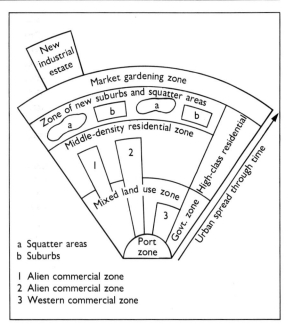

Fig. 5.8 Model of the main land use zones of large cities in South-East Asia.
Source: after McGee, 1967.

based on ethnic segregation – a notable feature also of many African cities but not those of Latin America where racial mixing has been more common.

Figure 5.8 indicates some of these features. During colonial times high-class residential areas were mainly reserved for Europeans, with other groups in 'middle density' areas or older housing near the port. Precise locations were influenced by such factors as nearness to work and the preference of Europeans for slightly higher land. Since independence, wealth has tended to replace ethnic origin as the main factor influencing residential location, though this has not resulted in very dramatic changes. Squatter settlements or other kinds of informal housing have resulted from recent rapid in-migration.

Problems have arisen in trying to find appropriate terminology for such settlements which, in many cases, are inhabited by people who are not technically squatters because they have legal rights of some kind to live where they do. This issue is discussed in more detail in Chapter 7 but the term 'informal housing' is useful to describe the wide range of housing constructed outside the formal building regulations either because it is built on land without the owner's permission or because it does not conform with the required legal standards regarding, for example, materials used or safety. In some cities, notably Singapore and Hong Kong, large-scale public housing projects have helped to restrict the growth of informal housing. Industry is still limited in most cities but industrial estates have been developed in the outer parts of many cities in recent years.

It is clear from this discussion of urban morphology that there is likely to be a close relationship between the configuration of the built environment and the residential distribution and residential mobility of the various social groups who inhabit a particular city. These two related topics are the subject of the next two chapters.

Ludlow: the changing morphology of an English country town

Small though it is, Ludlow in Shropshire (population about 8,000) possesses most of the characteristic morphological features of long-established towns and cities without having the daunting complexity of larger centres of this type such as York or Edinburgh, where, apart from their larger size, engulfment of once independent settlements and coalescence with others makes analysis more difficult.

Despite its small size, Ludlow has a long history. It was an important military fortress in the Norman period, a wool and cloth centre of the first rank throughout the medieval period, and for 200 years up to 1689 it was the seat of the Council of the Marches which virtually made it the capital of Wales and the border counties. Its early townscape is remarkably well

preserved. The town *kernel*, to use Smailes' terminology, lies in a loop of the River Teme at a bridging point on the ancient route from Shrewsbury to Bristol, the modern A49 (Fig. 5.9), a location that helped to secure its continued commercial importance as a market and coaching town once its strategic function as a military stronghold on the Welsh Marches had become redundant.

When viewed from the approach roads the town is still dominated by the commanding architectural presence of its parish church and the castle ruins, as it has been for hundreds of years. Once inside the kernel there is a distinctive historic feel in a townscape characterised by a tight network of rectilinear streets reflecting its origin as a planned Norman town, by occasional

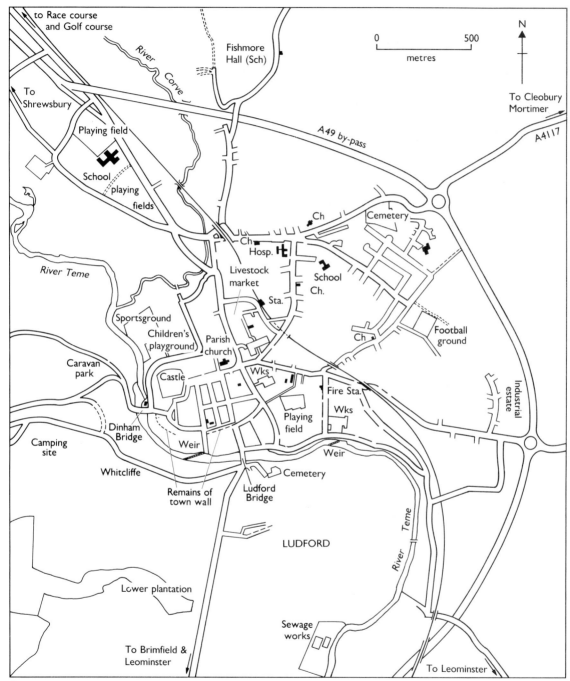

Fig. 5.9 Ludlow.

narrow yards and passages marking long
medieval properties with narrow street
frontages, and by the substantial number of

attractive medieval half-timbered and Georgian
brick and stone buildings. The evidence of
medieval properties reflects the town's import-

Fig. 5.10 The town kernel of Ludlow, dominated by its parish church, medieval half-timbered buildings and Georgian townhouses.

ance at that time in the wool and cloth trade, and the impressive Georgian buildings indicate its standing as a social centre in the 18th century (Fig. 5.10)

The River Teme prohibited any substantial growth to the west, and danger of flooding from the River Corve deflected expansion from the north-west. The town has therefore grown from its historic core in an arc running from the north, through east to south over what had been the town fields. The coming of the Shrewsbury to Hereford railway in 1851, with the station to the north-east of the old town, was an important catalyst in the further development of the townscape of the modern town. Between the old town and the railway – Smailes' *inner integuments* – there grew up between the mid-19th century and the First World War a mixed zone of terraces, workshops, small factories, chapels and public houses. Today, as in other towns and cities large and small, this is an area of change. It has a mixture of land uses, including a clothing factory in a converted chapel, the town's livestock market, a large supermarket, and an extensive municipal car park. Its townscape is untidy and unmemorable.

In the last 70 years the town has grown to the north-east and east, doubling its area in the process. This part of the town, which is predominantly residential, is characterised by detached and semi-detached houses along curving streets and culs-de-sac forming the familiar 'villa studding' townscape of the *outer integuments*. The recently completed by-pass, designed to ease traffic congestion in the old town, has attracted new industrial development to the urban periphery. The periphery is also marked by a number of other typical urban fringe features including a large school and its extensive playing fields, a sewage works, a cemetery, a golf course and Ludlow race course.

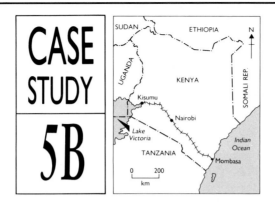

CASE STUDY 5B

Nairobi: urban morphology of a colonial city

Early growth and evolution of land use patterns

Urban settlements in Kenya are primarily products of the colonial era, though rapid growth has continued since Kenya's independence in 1963. Nairobi has grown most rapidly of all and is now a 'million city'. It originated in 1899 as a railway camp on the Mombasa–Kisumu railway but quickly developed as the railway headquarters and as an administrative centre. In 1907 it became the capital of Kenya and by 1914 its population exceeded 20,000. From the beginning, Nairobi's population was a mixture of ethnic groups. The few Europeans were outnumbered by Asians (from the Indian subcontinent) and Africans attracted by early employment opportunities. As in many other colonial cities, limitations were imposed on where non-Europeans could live, and distinctive land use zones soon emerged with residential land use based on ethnic segregation. The early patterns are still recognisable today (Fig. 5.11), though ethnic restrictions on land ownership no longer apply. It is interesting to compare present land use zones with McGee's model of land use in the colonial cities of South-East Asia. O'Connor (1983) has suggested that Nairobi is a special kind of African colonial city established primarily to meet the needs of European settlers. Lusaka and Harare are similar cities but

O'Connor views some other African colonial cities, such as Lagos and Kinshasa, as being more influenced by African decision-making and initiative than Nairobi.

Administrative, commercial and industrial areas

Administrative and commercial functions were soon concentrated in Nairobi's central area, a triangular zone limited by the railway to the south and west and the Nairobi River to the north-east. The railway route has since been altered, so the western boundary is now the Uhuru Highway, but the location of the zone remains unchanged (Fig. 5.11). A distinctive part of this zone includes the Parliament Buildings, ministerial offices and the Kenyatta Conference Centre which hosts many international meetings (Fig. 5.12). The university and various other educational and cultural buildings are in the northern part of the zone but the east of the triangle, sloping down towards the Nairobi River, contains much poor-quality commercial and residential building. This is comparable in function and, to some extent, appearance to the run-down inner-city fringes of many European cities.

South-east of the city centre is the main industrial zone, formalised by the 1948 Nairobi

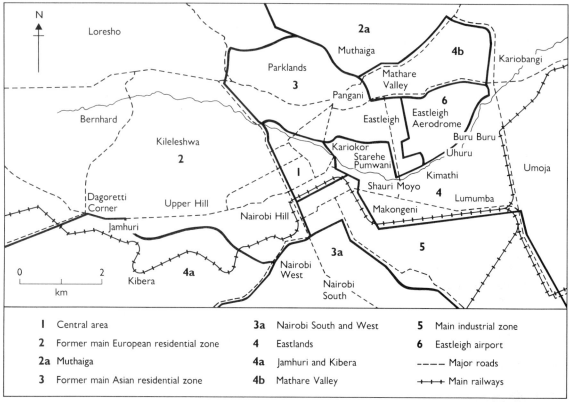

Fig. 5.11 Nairobi: land use zones.

1	Central area	3a	Nairobi South and West	5	Main industrial zone
2	Former main European residential zone	4	Eastlands	6	Eastleigh airport
2a	Muthaiga	4a	Jamhuri and Kibera	- - - -	Major roads
3	Former main Asian residential zone	4b	Mathare Valley	+++	Main railways

Fig. 5.12 Nairobi central area in the late 1980s. This view of the city centre from the west shows Uhuru Park, often used for open-air meetings, in the foreground. Beyond this can be seen the Kenyatta Conference Centre (the tallest building on the right of the photograph), the clock tower of the Parliament Building (adjacent to the Conference Centre), and various banks, offices and hotels.

Master Plan. Many of the industries are market-oriented, serving the varied needs of Nairobi's population. Most were initially dependent on local initiatives but major expansion in the last 20 years is evidenced particularly by the growth of multinational concerns. This 'formal' industrial area provides a striking contrast to the 'informal' industries scattered throughout poorer residential areas such as the Mathare Valley.

Residential land use before independence

Early development of housing for Europeans on Nairobi Hill, a pleasant, elevated area near the city centre, was gradually extended in the period before independence to provide estates for European residents throughout the western and northern periphery of the city. These consisted mainly of large, detached homes in extensive gardens with parks and wooded valleys providing additional open space. Asian residential areas were mainly on the northern side of the

Fig. 5.13 Pumwani estate in the early 1970s, shortly before demolition of the area began. Only an estimated one in every four of the inhabitants of Pumwani could afford to live in the alternative accommodation offered to them at the time of demolition. Many moved into the informal housing areas of the Mathare Valley because of this.

city between Parklands and Eastleigh, closer to the central area than the European estate of Muthaiga. Marked contrasts existed between the affluent housing of the Parklands area and the cheap, crowded dwellings typical of Eastleigh. During the 1950s new Asian estates (Nairobi South and Nairobi West) were constructed near the growing industrial zone.

Early African housing was largely unplanned, as at Pangani where it was demolished to be replaced by an Asian estate in the 1930s. Planned development, confined to Eastlands (Fig. 5.11), began with Pumwani estate in 1922. Blocks of land, with communal latrines and wash-houses constructed by the municipal council, were leased to landlords who allowed Africans to build their own homes, usually of mud-brick and thatch initially, on payment of a rent (Fig. 5.13). In neighbouring Kariokor and Starehe, housing was mainly provided by employers for their workers, much of it designed to accommodate three men in a room 3 m by 4 m. Family housing for Africans was rarely considered until after 1950, and in 1939 adult African males outnumbered females by a ratio of 8:1 in Nairobi.

Recent residential land use changes

As restrictions on land ownership by the different ethnic groups were withdrawn before and after independence in 1963, and as many Asians and Europeans left Kenya in the same period, Africans began to move into former Asian and European residences. Wealth and class replaced ethnicity as the determinants of where people could live. Today, the former European areas and the better areas of Asian housing remain the wealthy residential suburbs of the city, though no longer the preserve of particular ethnic groups.

Rapid in-migration to the city after 1950 created increased housing problems for the less affluent, however. Attempts to improve older formal housing in areas like Starehe and Kariokor and, from the late 1960s particularly, the building of new estates such as Uhuru and Kimathi in the east and Jamhuri and Kibera in the south-west,

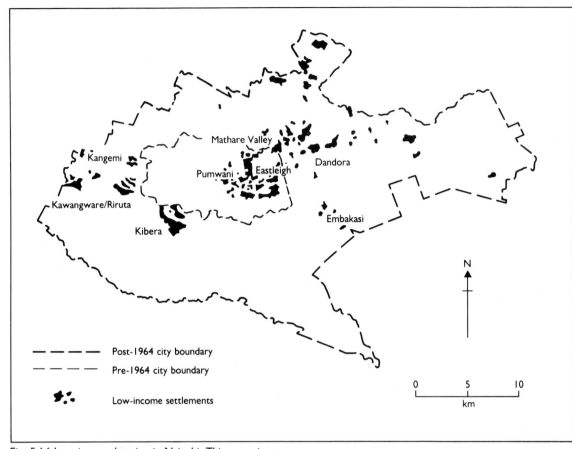

Fig. 5.14 Low-income housing in Nairobi. This map gives a useful indication of the extent of low-income settlements in Nairobi. Many of these are peripheral to the city. Most are informal housing areas but some, especially within the pre-1964 boundary, are areas of degraded formal housing.
Source: adapted from Lee-Smith and Memon, 1988.

failed to meet housing needs, with many people unable to afford to rent or buy homes provided by the formal sector. For many people, especially new migrants to the city, 'informal' housing was the only possibility. Since the 1950s there have been massive developments of different kinds of informal housing in areas like the Mathare Valley (where over 100,000 people occupy such accommodation) and the western periphery of the city (Fig. 5.14). Housing types vary from 'self-help' constructions using any available materials, to wooden sheds in which individual rooms may be rented. Most sites are peripheral because the city authorities have generally destroyed any attempts to develop informal housing near the city centre. There have been some attempts to develop site and service schemes (see Chapter 7) with help from various official and voluntary organisations in areas such as Dandora, but these have not been particularly successful – often because they prove too expensive for the very poor. In present economic circumstances it seems likely that as the city's population continues to grow, further areas of informal housing will be added to Nairobi's townscape.

6

The social geography of urban areas

Although references have been made to socially different residential areas and to the movement of social groups within towns and cities, these have been subsidiary concerns so far. They form the main subjects of this and the next chapter.

The spatial arrangement of social areas of various kinds in today's towns and cities displays a remarkable diversity and reflects their major periods of expansion, the different economic and cultural contexts in which they have evolved, including their pre-modern legacy, and the roles played by national and local governments in their development.

The classical models

Concentric zone model

The earliest and most widely known attempt to generalise about the social geography of a modern city is Ernest Burgess's so-called 'concentric zone model', based on a study of Chicago and published in 1924. His model was concerned with urban growth as well as social areas and may be summarised in his own words: 'the expansion of the city can best be illustrated, perhaps, by a series of concentric circles, which may be numbered to designate both the successive zones of urban extension and the types of areas differentiated in the process of expansion'.

The model contains five zones (Fig. 6.1). At the centre (zone 1) is the Central Business District (CBD); surrounding the CBD is a zone of factories and slums (zone 2), the latter containing distinct ethnic districts. Zone 3 consists of working-class people's homes, beyond which lie an extensive residential zone (zone 4) and a

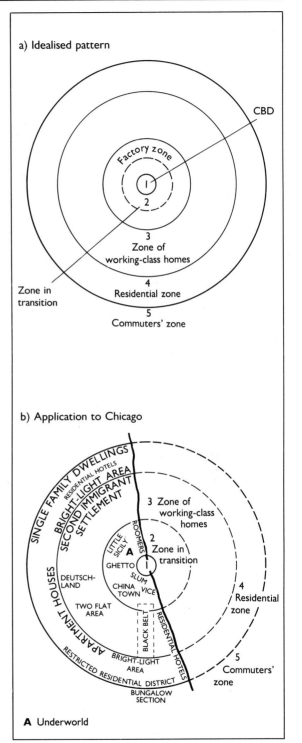

Fig. 6.1 Burgess's concentric zone model.
Source: Park, Burgess and McKenzie, 1925.

commuters' zone (zone 5). Expansion of the city takes place through the twin processes of *invasion* and *succession*, terms borrowed from plant ecology and applied to human populations. Burgess envisaged the CBD gradually encroaching on the run-down residential/industrial districts surrounding it which in turn, if population growth continued, would expand into the working-class residential areas, and so on throughout the whole of the urban area. Although the model appears to be concerned primarily with differences in socio-economic status, it is also obviously related to ethnic origins and lifestyle (that is, it would be expected that there would be far more single people in zone 2 than in zones 3 to 5, where nuclear families would be the norm).

Since its publication, Burgess's model has been the subject of much criticism and reappraisal. Two important criticisms of the model are that it is 'culture-bound' and 'time-dependent'. It only relates, say the critics, to large, rapidly growing cities containing heterogeneous populations and with important commercial and industrial economies developed in a free-enterprise system. Such cities were common throughout North America in the early 20th century. The model is less likely to be relevant to cities with declining, relatively homogeneous populations and in which housing construction is controlled in part or totally by central or local government.

Sector model

In 1939 Homer Hoyt, a land economist, presented an alternative model which has become known as the 'sector model'. Hoyt's model arose out of his work for the US Federal Housing Administration by whom he was employed to classify areas in American cities according to their mortgage lending risk. Unlike Burgess's study which was based on a long association with one city, Hoyt analysed housing characteristics in 142 American cities. He suggested that once a particular land use developed outside the CBD, it tended to grow outwards, as the city grew, along a particular axis or axes. He pointed out that the areas of most desirable housing tended to be located in one or more sectors. On either side of these sectors would be found housing areas of intermediate quality. Poor housing occupied

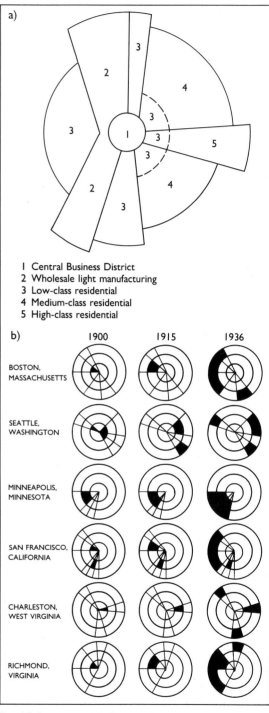

1 Central Business District
2 Wholesale light manufacturing
3 Low-class residential
4 Medium-class residential
5 High-class residential

Fig. 6.2 Sector model. *Source*: Hoyt, 1939.
a) Hoyt's sector model.
b) The sectoral movement of the most desirable residential areas in six American cities.

quite separate sectors which also extended from the centre to the periphery (Fig 6.2a). Figure 6.2b shows the changing location of the most desirable residential areas, as identified by Hoyt, in six American cities between 1900 and 1936. Outward sectoral movement is clearly evident in these examples. Such fashionable residential areas were, according to Hoyt, likely to be found on high ground, along major transport routes leading to open country, along waterfronts not used by industry, and in the direction of the houses of leaders of the community.

Multiple nuclei model

The third, and last, of the so-called 'classical' models was devised by two geographers, Harris and Ullman, in 1945 (Fig. 6.3). Unlike the models already discussed, which assume that a city evolves from one nucleus, the Harris and Ullman model allows for the fact that a city may evolve from a number of quite separate nuclei – hence its popular name, the 'multiple nuclei model'. The authors envisaged commercial,

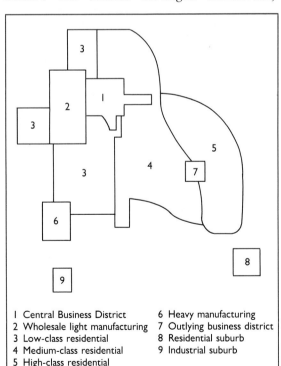

1 Central Business District	6 Heavy manufacturing
2 Wholesale light manufacturing	7 Outlying business district
3 Low-class residential	8 Residential suburb
4 Medium-class residential	9 Industrial suburb
5 High-class residential	

Fig. 6.3 Multiple nuclei model.
Source: Harris and Ullman, 1959.

industrial and residential nodes which eventually fuse to form the metropolitan area. These nuclei are created and grow as a result of the locational needs of different land users, their ability to pay rents, and the desire of some users to be distant from others (for example, high-class residential areas will be distant from heavy industry). Harris and Ullman did acknowledge that cities were so varied that their internal structure was unlikely to be accounted for by one model and that a combination of zones, sectors and nuclei was likely to be found in most cities. This is a matter to which we shall return in due course.

Social area analysis

Another approach to analysing the structure of the city was put forward in the late 1940s and early 1950s by three sociologists working on the west coast of the USA. It combines a theory and a technique and may be seen as a 'bridge' between the earlier classical models and the quantitative techniques of urban analysis widely used in the 1960s and 1970s. The approach is called 'social area analysis' and was developed by Shevky, Williams and Bell. It is based on three contemporary trends that the authors suggested were taking place in modern society and which were mirrored in the city:

1) Increasing sorting of society on the basis of socio-economic status (they called this *social rank*).
2) The weakening of traditional family structure, for example the increasing number of women with jobs and careers outside the home (*urbanisation*).
3) Increasing sorting according to ethnic type (*segregation*).

These three expressions of social change – social rank, urbanisation and segregation – they called *constructs*. Having identified them they set out to measure them using census data at the census tract level. (A census tract is a small area into which US urban areas are subdivided for census purposes. The average population size of a census tract is 4,000.)

Social rank was measured by gathering data relating to occupation and education; urbanisation was measured by collecting data on fertility, the number of women at work, and the number of single family homes; and segregation was measured simply by recording the proportion of ethnic minority groups in the total population of a census tract.

The data for each census tract were then averaged and standardised on a score from 0 to 100. For social rank a low score indicates an area populated predominantly by persons with poor levels of education and employed in unskilled, manual jobs. High scores indicate areas populated by people with university or equivalent qualifications employed in professional and managerial capacities. For urbanisation a low score indicates an area composed largely of nuclear families living in single-family houses with the wives not in employment. High scores indicate areas with many apartments housing a large unmarried population with a high proportion of the adult female population in employment. The social rank and urbanisation scores were then subdivided into four categories and portrayed on a so-called *social space diagram*. This gave 16 social area types. Those census tracts with an above average tract minority population were then indicated on the diagram. This gives a total of 32 possible social area types in all (16 types based on social rank and urbanisation, each of which may have a segregated ethnic minority). Figure 6.4 shows the application of social area analysis to the Canadian city of Winnipeg.

Factorial ecology

Social area analysis came under criticism from a number of other researchers in the 1950s and 1960s. Among criticisms of the approach were the subjectivity of the choice of census data used, and the fact that the theoretical basis of the approach was suspect when applied to urbanisation outside North America. Despite these criticisms a number of studies were made in the late 1950s and 1960s, designed not only to test the validity of the approach in theoretical terms but also to map and generalise about the distribution of social areas based on social rank, urbanisation and levels of segregation. It was during this period that sophisticated computers became available to those engaged in urban research. This technical advance not only enabled large amounts of data to be used but also allowed, by using a statistical technique called *factor analysis*, greater objectivity. This is achieved by submitting a large range of census variables to statistical analysis. This allows the most important social dimensions to be recognised and these are named according to the census variables which contribute most to them. For example, in a study of Winnipeg using factor analysis, 34 census variables were used (including such diverse measures as percentage of population under five years, percentage of owner-occupiers, percentage of recent immigrants, percentage of British origin, number of persons per room, percentage of women at work, and percentage Roman Catholic) for each of the 86 census tracts in the city. An analysis of urban social areas using factor analysis is called *factorial ecology*.

It is beyond the scope of this book to explain in detail the factor analysis technique. What is important is to outline the findings of the studies using the technique and to show the relationship of these findings to earlier studies. Although there are regional variations, factorial ecologies of North American cities generally confirm the social area analysis constructs of social rank (now usually called socio-economic status), urbanisation (now usually referred to as family status or family life cycle), and segregation. Moreover, the evidence also suggests that socio-economic status is arranged in sectors, family status in concentric zones, and ethnic minorities in clusters.

Studies of factorial ecology in North America thus suggest that it is possible to combine the classical models of zones, sectors and nuclei with the constructs of social area analysis into a comprehensive view of urban social structure. This is well illustrated in a schematic diagram of urban residential structure resulting from a study of the Canadian city of Toronto (Fig. 6.5). The suggestion is that the social geography of a North American city is an amalgam of sectors, zones and clusters, but that this simple geometrical arrangement will be distorted by the accidents of history and the peculiarities of the sites of particular cities. The application of this model to Chicago, based on 1960 census data, is described in Case Study 6.

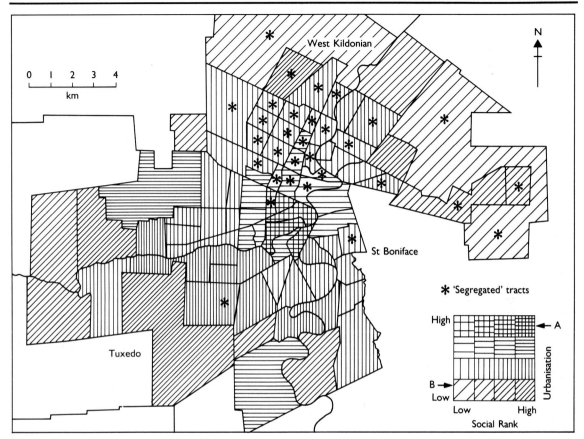

Fig. 6.4 Social areas in Winnipeg, 1961. The square in the bottom right-hand corner is a *social space diagram* showing 16 social area types. Type A areas are of high social rank and high urbanisation. Such areas will normally be in that sector of the city where other affluent people live, but usually in the inner part of that sector, because 'high urbanised' means there will be many single adults, and such people value access to the city centre above the spaciousness of suburban homes and gardens. The map shows that there were only two type A areas in Winnipeg in 1961 and they were both at the apex of a sector of high social rank stretching southwards from the centre of the city. Type B areas are of low social rank and low urbanisation. These are working-class areas with families with children, and mothers not working outside the home in most cases. In Winnipeg such areas were in the north and north-east. These type B areas were also described as 'segregated'. In Winnipeg in 1961 this denoted concentrations of Roman Catholics and French Canadians.
Source: Herbert, 1972.

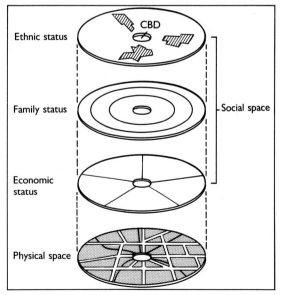

Fig. 6.5 The residential structure of the North American city, based on factorial ecology of Toronto.
Source: Murdie, 1969.

Urban social geographies outside North America

In cities that have evolved in economic, political and cultural contexts not unlike those of the USA and Canada, similar patterns to those found in North America may be expected to be found; in rather different cultures and economic and political contexts, variations are likely. For example, studies of Copenhagen and Helsinki have produced broadly similar results to North American studies in that in both cities socio-economic status and family status were important in shaping their social geographies, though ethnicity was of negligible importance. A study of Melbourne, Australia, identified socio-economic status, family status and ethnic origin (that is, areas dominated by immigrants from southern Europe) as the most important dimensions.

British cities, although containing identifiable sectors of varying socio-economic status and zones of differing family status, have been shown to display important deviations from the North American model, largely because a significant proportion (as high as 40 per cent in some cases) of the housing stock is council housing. People in council housing move less often than owner-occupiers, local authorities often attempt to build mixed developments rather than separate the young from the old, and council developments occur in all types of locations – in the centre and on the periphery, and in high-status and low-status sectors. For all these reasons the social structure of British cities is unique. Figure 6.6 is an attempt to generalise about the social structure of a British city. It combines sectors based on social status and concentric zones based on age differences (family status) but with distortions related to the presence of council housing. In the model the highest-status sector runs south from the centre. At its northern end just outside the central commercial area there is a very mixed population of very low-paid young families, immigrant households, students and young professionals, predominantly in large, subdivided houses. Council tenants live both in the inner city and on the periphery and in all but the very highest-status sectors. In some council-dominated areas, old and young families, old-age pensioners and relatively young single people live in close proximity, for example in the

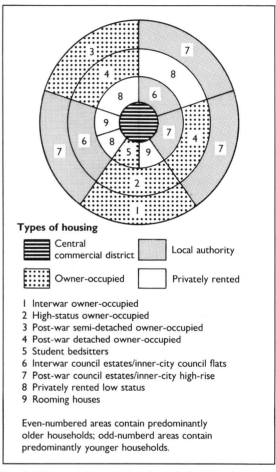

Types of housing

▤ Central commercial district	▨ Local authority
▧ Owner-occupied	☐ Privately rented

1 Interwar owner-occupied
2 High-status owner-occupied
3 Post-war semi-detached owner-occupied
4 Post-war detached owner-occupied
5 Student bedsitters
6 Interwar council estates/inner-city council flats
7 Post-war council estates/inner-city high-rise
8 Privately rented low status
9 Rooming houses

Even-numbered areas contain predominantly older households; odd-numberd areas contain predominantly younger households.

Fig. 6.6 The social geography of an idealised medium-sized British city.
Source: Robson, 1975.

inner-city council housing areas to the east and north-east of the commercial core.

Beyond Western Europe and other areas of 'West European' culture (for example Australasia), there are greater deviations from the North American pattern, for example in the largely rebuilt cities of Eastern Europe and in the Third World. Studies of social geography in the Third World have been limited, partly because of problems of data availability and reliability. Berry and Rees (1969) in a study based on 37 census variables for Calcutta, saw the city as being in a transitional state between that of a

Exercise 6.1

Aspects of the social geography of Sheffield

Study the table on page 82 which shows selected socio-economic indicators for six wards in the city of Sheffield in 1980. The locations of the wards are shown on the accompanying map.

a) Compare and contrast the inner-city wards of Castle and Park.

b) Compare and contrast the two outer wards of Hallam and Mosborough.

c) The populations of Park and Hallam wards are almost identical, yet Hallam is many times bigger than Park. In what ways would you expect the townscapes of these two wards to differ?

d) The 'concentric zone' model of Burgess, and later social area analysis and factorial ecology studies, have suggested that the outer urban ring will be populated by young families, and the middle ring by older families. To what extent are these generalisations upheld by the evidence presented here?

e) Refer back to Fig. 6.6 which shows an idealised medium-sized British city. To which of the nine types of area incorporated in that model do (i) Park, and (ii) Hallam, most closely correspond? Give reasons for your answer.

pre-industrial and industrial city with elements of modernity present (for example increasing land use specialisation), but with many traditional features remaining. Social contrasts included that between the many single males, including numerous pavement dwellers with no proper houses, in the mixed land use zone of the central area, and the more stable, established family groupings of the areas further from the centre. A notable ethnic element was the association of high levels of female employment with Muslim areas, a reflection of varying attitudes to female employment by different religious groups.

Urban ethnic segregation

The presence of sizeable ethnic minorities (defined in terms of race, religion or national origin) is a common characteristic of cities and this is reflected in their significant place in generalisations made about the overall social spatial structure of such cities. However, it would be wrong to assume that ethnic clusters are static, permanent and homogeneous. Such areas may contract in size, may grow in particular ways and directions, may disappear altogether after a period of time, and may contain diverse groups in terms of origin and social status.

Almost all ethnic minority groups were originally in-migrants (migrants from other parts of the same country, for example Blacks in Chicago, Catholics in Belfast), or immigrants (migrants from another country, for example Puerto Ricans in New York, West Indians in London, Jews in North African cities, Chinese in South-East Asian cities). Over time, of course, an increasing proportion of an ethnic minority which was originally immigrant will be native-born, but this will not necessarily result in residential dispersal. Figure 6.7 shows the variety of spatial outcomes that emerge when a minority group enters an urban area. If the ethnic minority has few differences from the receiving (host) society, then rapid, or indeed instant, dispersal is

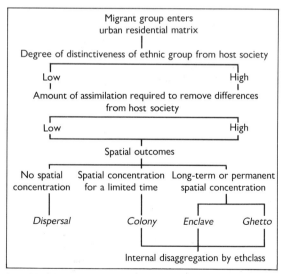

Fig. 6.7 Ethnic groups: assimilation and residential spatial outcomes.
Source: Boal, 1976.

1981 Census: Key indicators for selected Sheffield wards. *Source*: Office of Population Censuses and Surveys.

	1	2	3	4	5	6	7	8	9	10	11	12	13	14	15	16	17
		Persons			Pop. with head born in New Commonwealth	Children in lone adult families	Pensioner alone	Unemployed		Households 3+ children	Renting	Not in self-contained accommodation	>1 person per room	Lack/share bath	No car	Census usually resident	Number of households
	0-4	5-15	60/65+	75+				Men	Women								
Castle	7.2	16.4	16.6	4.7	8.0	9.1	38.2	26.3	12.0	7.6	81.3	0.4	6.6	3.4	73.3	19203	7350
Hallam	5.1	14.6	20.9	7.3	1.6	2.6	30.3	5.3	3.5	5.2	18.2	0.1	0.7	2.0	30.6	17709	6824
Heeley	4.8	15.3	20.2	6.6	3.6	5.4	33.4	13.0	6.4	5.2	48.0	1.0	2.8	5.9	54.4	19244	7508
Mosborough	6.5	18.0	15.0	3.9	0.5	4.8	27.7	12.3	6.9	7.0	61.8	–	3.7	2.1	44.4	22433	8016
Nether Edge	5.7	13.5	18.4	6.7	9.4	4.3	32.0	11.7	6.8	6.4	28.2	4.8	2.1	8.8	44.8	16340	6479
Park	4.5	13.3	25.0	7.1	1.0	8.5	35.3	18.9	8.3	3.9	91.8	–	3.8	1.0	70.4	17558	7404
SHEFFIELD	5.1	15.7	19.9	6.3	3.2	5.5	32.9	14.0	7.1	5.8	55.5	0.7	3.3	3.1	51.8	530843	203145

Notes Columns 1–4 are expressed as percentages of the usually resident population (column 16).

Columns 10–15 are expressed as percentages of the number of private households (column 17).

Column 6 shows the number of children in lone adult households as a percentage of the total number of children aged 0–15 (columns 1 and 2)

Columns 8 and 9 are expressed as percentages of the number of economically active persons in each sex.

Column 5 shows the number of persons in households whose head was born in the New Commonwealth or Pakistan as a percentage of the usually resident population (column 16).

Column 7 shows the number of pensioner households as a percentage of the total number of pensioners (column 3).

likely to occur, for example British immigrants to Australian cities. If there are marked differences between the newcomers and the host society then, initially, concentration is likely to occur. In some cases this is short-lived, for instance until language difficulties have been overcome, in which case the term *colony* is used to describe the ethnic cluster. In other cases, where ethnic distinctiveness is marked (for example colour, religious practices, social customs), then concentration and segregation are likely to occur, which may be long-term or permanent.

The factors leading to long-term segregation may be grouped under two headings: internal and external. *Internal factors* include strong ethnic institutions such as places of worship, schools, approved food shops and mutual benefit societies. *External factors* include lack of access to well-rewarded occupations and to certain types of housing or housing areas. Where the strength of ethnic institutions is the dominant factor influencing segregation, it is usual to refer to the resultant concentrations as *enclaves*. Where external factors are dominant, the term *ghetto* is used. In practice, it is not always easy to distinguish between enclaves and ghettos, as many concentrations have arisen and are perpetuated by a combination of internal and external factors. These are referred to as *enclave-ghettos*.

Ethnic concentrations, whether colonies, enclaves or ghettos, begin predominantly in inner-city locations. Reasons for this include access to the cheapest accommodation and to a variety of service and manufacturing jobs in the central commercial area and neighbouring industrial districts. Subsequently they may assume a variety of spatial forms. These are summarised in Figure 6.8. Area A represents an area formerly occupied by an ethnic minority who have now been assimilated into the host society; the concentration has, therefore, ceased to exist. Area B represents an enclave-ghetto occupied by an ethnic minority whose numbers are growing only very slowly and who occupy a lowly socio-economic position; they therefore reside in a small, static, inner-city cluster. Areas C(i)–(iii) are the successive locations of the homes of a fairly homogeneous ethnic minority who have increased their socio-economic status over time and whose ethnic institutions have remained strong. They now occupy a high-status

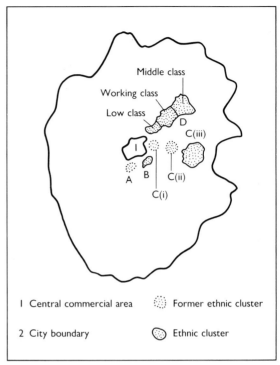

Fig. 6.8 Types of ethnic cluster. (See text for explanation.)

enclave on the urban periphery. Area D shows the area occupied by an ethnic minority whose numbers continue to grow rapidly, in which there are considerable variations in socio-economic status, and where external factors have prevented the most affluent members from dispersing into the rest of the urban area. This is therefore an enclave-ghetto (but much nearer the ghetto end of the enclave-ghetto continuum) in the form of a truncated sector. Different socio-economic groups occupy different parts of the sector, with the poorest in the inner city and the most affluent near the periphery. Such socio-economic divisions within ethnic clusters are called *ethclass divisions*. These generalisations may be partly illustrated by the examples of Blacks in Detroit and Roman Catholics in Belfast.

Ethnic segregation in Detroit

Where members of minorities, such as the Blacks in American cities, are prevented by various means from dispersing and where many, anyway, would not wish to leave areas occupied

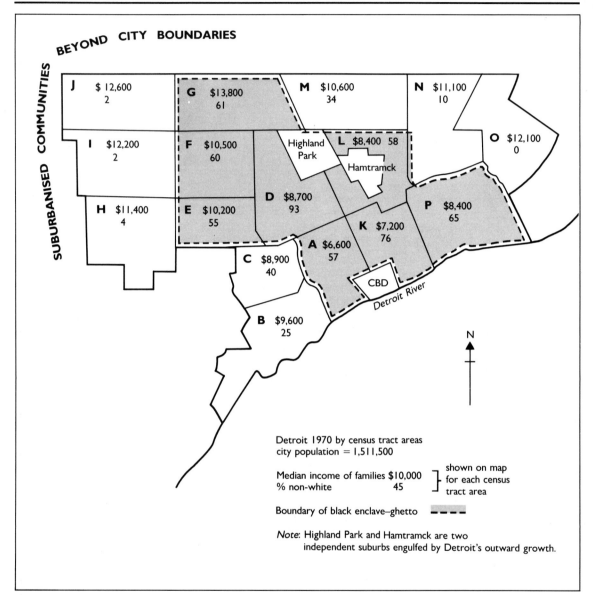

Fig. 6.9 The black ghetto in Detroit, 1970.
Source: based on US Bureau of Census data.

predominantly by that minority, it is to be expected that marked ethclass divisions will occur. This is clearly illustrated in Detroit, where almost 45 per cent of the 1.5 million inhabitants in 1970 were Blacks. Figure 6.9 shows that the Black ghetto (or more properly the enclave-ghetto) in 1970, defined as census tract areas more than 50 per cent Black, formed a truncated sector. Just outside the CBD, in census tract area A, the median family income was only $6,600.

Surrounding this area were others with median family incomes between $7,000 and $10,000. It should be noted that census tract area G had the highest median family income in the whole of the city. Despite increased Black suburbanisation to smaller communities beyond the city boundary in the last 20 years, Detroit's Black population has continued to rise, and the ghetto with its internal class divisions has continued to expand.

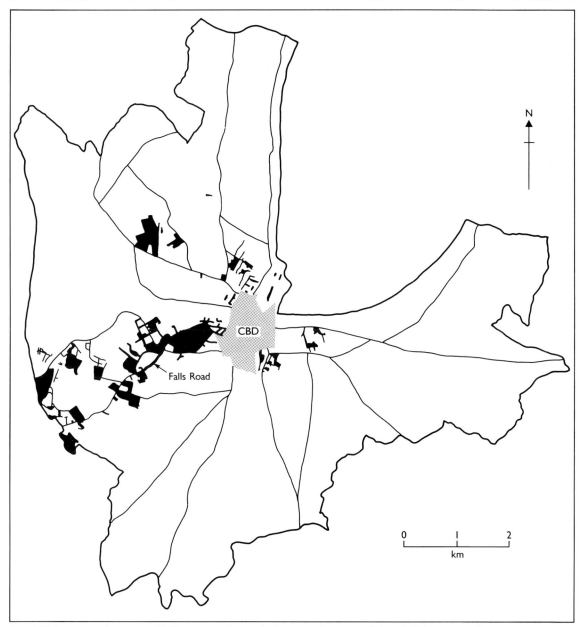

Fig. 6.10 Location of streets in Belfast county borough that were between 90.5 and 100 per cent Catholic in mid-1969. *Source*: after Poole and Boal, 1973.

Segregation in Belfast

Figure 6.10 shows the distribution of a partly segregated minority in a British city. It shows the distribution of streets that were between 90.5 per cent and 100 per cent Catholic in Belfast in mid-1969. This was before the present troubles and represents a situation after several decades of relative calm. The Catholics had retained a highly distinctive identity, due in part to their religious practices and their nationalist sympathies (in a 1970 survey, 76 per cent of Belfast's

Catholics considered themselves to be Irish; 75 per cent of the Protestants regarded themselves to be British or Ulstermen/women) and in part to discrimination in the field of housing. However, it should be noted that 44 per cent of Catholic households in mid-1969 lived outside the segregated areas shown on the map. It should also be noted that segregated living is an entrenched feature of Protestant working-class areas in the city as well.

The map shows that almost all of the segregated Catholics lived in a small number of distinct areas. To the north and east of the CBD, these were relatively small and formed a discontinuous zone around the city centre. The largest area, developed along the Falls Road, formed a more or less continuous sector stretching westwards from the edge of the city to the urban periphery. This sectoral development is typical of a situation where an ethnic minority has been present for a long time and is experiencing continued population growth. Since the late 1960s further polarisation of the two communities has taken place. It has been estimated that from 1969 to 1973, between 8,000 and 15,000 families left mixed neighbourhoods and went to live in segregated areas. Segregation levels fell between 1971 and 1981 in some inner areas mainly as a result of general population decline, but the Falls Road sector became even more segregated.

Apartheid in South Africa

Ethnic segregation was a feature of many African cities during colonial times but rapid changes have usually occurred after independence, as in Harare, Zimbabwe's capital, and Nairobi (see Case Study 5B). Today, South Africa's urban areas still provide an extreme example of ethnic segregation. Legislation, most notably the Group Areas Act of 1950, has been used to enforce the residential segregation of whites, Blacks, coloureds (people of mixed race), and Indians, in keeping with the government's *apartheid* policies. Ghetto-like constraints have been imposed on all the non-white groups. Results of this include the growth of large peripheral Black 'cities', of which Soweto in the Johannesburg conurbation is the best known, and the eviction of families who contravene the Group Areas Act by trying to settle in an area other than that allocated to their own group. Rule (1989) suggests that implementation of this Act in an attempt to maintain racial segregation has faced some difficulties in the late 1980s, and some 'grey' areas with a mixture of racial groups have developed in Johannesburg, Cape Town and other cities. The extent to which racially integrated areas develop in future will, however, be dependent on changes in the political situation and related legislation.

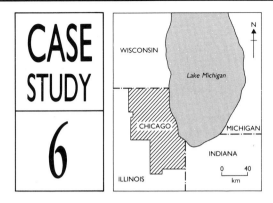

CASE STUDY 6

The social geography of Chicago

The social geography of Chicago, one of the world's largest metropolitan areas with a population in excess of 10 million, has been the subject of a great deal of attention in the last 70 years. A close study of changes taking place there in the early decades of the 20th century was the basis of Burgess's *concentric zone theory* of urban social differentiation and spatial growth, published in 1924. His pioneering study was followed in the late 1920s and 1930s by a series of detailed monographs by his followers, analysing specific social areas such as the Jewish ghetto, the affluent 'Gold Coast' along the shores of Lake Michigan in the north of the city, the 'rooming-house' areas, and 'Little Sicily' where many migrants from southern Italy were concentrated. More recently Berry and Rees (1969) have completed a comprehensive investigation of the social geography of the metropolis (in 1960), using factor analysis.

These two authors were not just investigating the social geography of the *city* of Chicago, but the whole Chicago *metropolitan area*. A metropolitan area is akin to a *conurbation* or a metropolitan county of the kind that existed in the UK between 1974 and 1984, such as the West Midlands or West Yorkshire. This is illustrated in Fig. 6.11, which shows Chicago metropolitan area in 1960. It is not one administrative unit but well over a thousand! It is made up of the city of Chicago, together with Cook county (much reduced in size because of

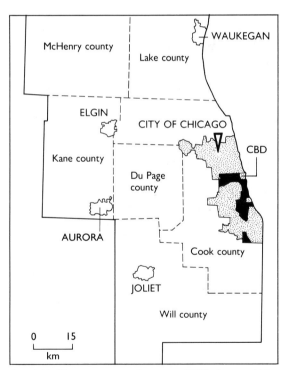

Fig. 6.11 Chicago metropolitan area, 1960. Areas within the city of Chicago with populations more than 50 per cent Black in 1960 are shaded, and the four industrial satellites of Waukegan, Elgin, Aurora and Joliet are indicated.

the growth of the city of Chicago), McHenry county, Lake county, Kane county, Du Page county and Will county. Within these six counties there are over a thousand towns and cities *independent* of the city of Chicago and of the

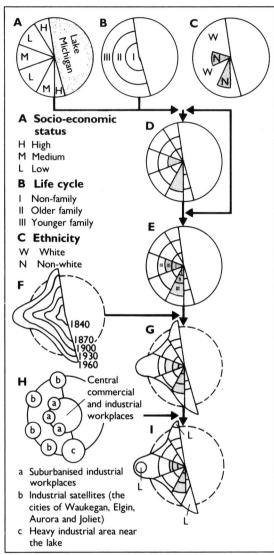

A **Socio-economic
   status**
H High
M Medium
L Low

B **Life cycle**
I   Non-family
II Older family
III Younger family

C **Ethnicity**
W White
N Non-white

a Suburbanised industrial
  workplaces
b Industrial satellites (the
  cities of Waukegan, Elgin,
  Aurora and Joliet)
c Heavy industrial area near
  the lake

Fig. 6.12 The social geography of Chicago.
Source: Berry and Rees, 1969.

of their generalised maps. However, Chicago is a lakeside metropolis, so the first distortion is that it is portrayed as a semi-circle. Maps A–C indicate in generalised form the sectors of socio-economic status, the zones of differing family status, and the ethnic (in this case non-white) clusters. At this stage the authors do not take into account any distorting features other than Chicago's lakeside location. These maps are, therefore, at a very high level of generality. Note that the lakeside locations have been occupied by high-class residential areas – as Hoyt suggested they would be if industrial development did not take place there. Map D shows the composite pattern that emerges when these three independent patterns are laid over one another. Map E shows the subdivision of the non-white clusters into zones according to family status – with single people in the inner zones, ageing families in the middle zones and young families in the newer housing in the outer zone – as in the rest of the metropolitan area. At this point the unique physical growth of the metropolis (F) and its peculiar industrial development (H) are brought into play to produce maps G and I, which bring the picture closer to reality. Of particular note on the final map is the way that the existence of a heavy industrial area at the lakeside in the south has terminated the growth of a high-class residential sector and resulted in the growth of a low-class housing area near to this major source of employment. This is reminiscent of Harris and Ullman's multiple nuclei model. Similar distortions have occurred on the western and northern peripheries of the metropolitan area.

In spite of the introduction of growth patterns and industrial districts which bring the initial severely geometrical patterns nearer to reality, it is important to emphasise the high degree of generalisation that still remains in models of this kind. This is illustrated in Fig. 6.11 which shows those community areas in Chicago metropolitan area with populations more than 50 per cent Black in 1960, together with the four satellite cities of Waukegan, Elgin, Aurora and Joliet. This map should be carefully compared with Fig. 6.12.

counties in which they lie. Many of the independent communities are small, but some – such as Waukegan, Elgin, Aurora and Joliet – have populations of over 70,000. The vast city region stretches for 135 km from north to south and 80 km from east to west.

Bearing in mind that we are concerned with a city region rather than just the major city at its hub, attention can now be turned to Berry and Rees's study, the summary maps for which are shown in Fig. 6.12. They use a circle as the basis

7

Urban housing and residential mobility

The generalisations concerning the social geography of cities in different parts of the world discussed in the last chapter present static stiuations. In reality they are 'stills' from an ever-changing picture. One-third of British households move every five years and in the USA, where on average each person moves 12 times in a lifetime, one-fifth of households move every year. These moves, while reflecting individual household choices and preferences, also involve landowners, developers, estate agents, financial institutions and local and central governments.

Mobility in cities in the developed world

Why people want to move

Recent studies suggest that most household moves are the result of two main groups of factors: those concerned with career changes, and those related to stages in the life cycle.

Career reasons (for example promotion, change of career) are very important in long-distance moves. It has long been recognised that each individual's life is marked by a number of distinct stages. Figure 7.1 shows an American interpretation of the way in which each stage, from young adulthood onwards, is accompanied by certain

	Percentage of households in each sample	Reason given
Bedminister	70	Marriage/to own a house
	13	Change in household size
St George	66	Marriage/to own a house
	12	Change in household size
	12	Troublesome neighbours
Westbury	28	Change in household size
	23	To own a house
	10	Previous residence was only temporary
St Pauls	21	Forced to move
	21	Setting up new household
	20	Changing space requirement
	12	Last place too expensive
	10	Poor physical condition of previous dwelling

Note Reasons accounting for less than 5% of responses are not included.

Fig. 7.2 Main reasons for moving into and within four residential areas in Bristol. *Source*: Short, 1978.

Stage	Access	Space	Median tenure	Housing age	Mobility	Locational preference
Pre-child	Important	Unimportant	Rented flat		1 move to own home	Centre city
Child bearing	Less important	Increasingly important	Rented house	Old	High: 2–3 moves	Middle and outer rings of centre city
Child rearing	Not important	Important	Owned	Relatively new	1 move to owned home	Periphery of city or suburbs
Child launching	Not important	Very important	Owned	New	1 move to second home	Suburbs
Post-child	Not important	Unimportant	Owned	New when first bought	Unlikely to move	
Later life	Not important	Unimportant	Widow leaves owned home to live with grown child			

Fig. 7.1 Stages in the family life cycle, and associated housing and locational preferences.
Source: Morgan, 1976.

family characteristics and preferences. It should be noted that in the USA, public housing (what in the UK is called council housing) represents only 2 per cent of all housing stock. In countries in which public housing represents a large proportion of the housing stock, a substantial number of households will live their entire lives in public rented property. In socialist countries this may be true of almost the entire population.

Figure 7.2 indicates the significance of life-cycle reasons in a recent study of moves into and within four contrasting areas in Bristol. Although some categories are a little ambiguous, the importance of the creation of a new household on marriage and the effects of increasing and decreasing family size cannot be doubted.

Mobility processes

Many people who wish to move, come to terms with their existing housing space or environment and so do not move. In Britain, for example, surveys have revealed that of the roughly 30 per cent of households that say they wish to move, only 10 per cent do move. The 'stayers' fall into two categories: those who lower their aspirations and put up with their present accommodation, and those who set about improving their accommodation and surrounding environment. In the latter case it may involve making alterations, for example by installing central heating or building an extension, or taking steps to improve their neighbourhood, for example by pressing for improved play space or campaigning for 'housing improvement area' status.

If these two courses of action are not acceptable, households will begin to search for a new home. The sources of information used by potential movers wishing to rent or buy property in the private sector vary enormously. In Britain, informal sources, such as 'looking around' and learning about possible new homes from friends and relatives are as important as advertisements in newspapers and information provided by estate agents. Informal sources are particularly important for home seekers at the lower end of the market.

The importance of informal sources suggests that people are more likely to search neighbourhoods if, first, they are familiar with those

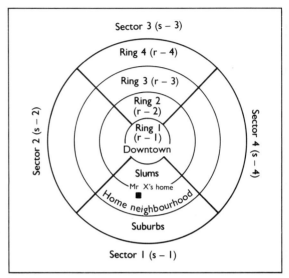

Fig. 7.3 Directional bias in residential mobility. *Source*: after Adams, 1969.

neighbourhoods and, secondly, if they think the area is residentially 'desirable' (a term much loved by estate agents). John Adams, an American geographer, suggested in 1969 that this is related to the 'mental map' that each person has of the city in which he or she lives. Adams' ideas are summarised in Fig. 7.3. Mr X is more familiar with sector 1 (s-1) in his city than any other; indeed the further he moves away from s-1 the more fuzzy his knowledge becomes. Within s-1 he is most familiar with ring-3 (r-3), in which he lives. He regards r-2, through which he travels to work each day, as an undesirable place in which to live. It is an area of mixed land uses and of deteriorating and densely packed housing. On the other hand he would regard a move to r-4, through which he travels on his way out of the city, as a 'step upward'. There the housing is modern, luxuriously appointed and set in large grounds.

Another important concept is suggested by Fig. 7.3. If Mr X were to move to r-4, then his home in r-3 will become available. This may provide an opportunity for a household living in r-2 to move to r-3. This would then release housing space in r-2, perhaps for a newly formed household with limited financial resources. This process is known as *filtering*. As intra-urban residential mobility takes place, houses tend to filter down and people tend to filter up. The working of the process is summarised in Fig. 7.4. There are

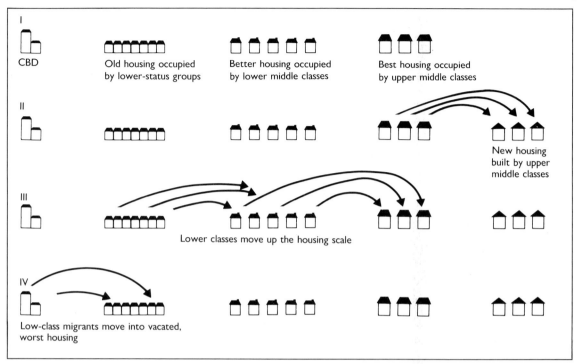

CBD

Old housing occupied
by lower-status groups

Better housing occupied
by lower middle classes

Best housing occupied
by upper middle classes

New housing
built by upper
middle classes

Lower classes move up the housing scale

Low-class migrants move into vacated,
worst housing

Fig. 7.4 The filtering process: simplified cross-section through a city, from CBD to periphery.
Source: Johnston, 1971.

exceptions to this general rule, however. In some cities former working-class housing is 'colonised' by middle-class households; in these cases the houses filter up. This process, called *gentrification*, has been particularly widespread in certain parts of inner London in such areas as Greenwich, Islington and Camberwell.

Urban 'gatekeepers'

So far the focus has been on the individual household faced with changing family circumstances, deciding whether or not to search for a new home, and then going about that search using a number of information sources and personal knowledge of the city. But this is less than half the story. Many households have very little choice, in that they may be renting public housing or seeking to rent such housing. These households will have decisions made for them. If families already renting housing in England and Wales, for example, wish to move, they will have to make a case to a local housing department official. If the transfer is agreed, the household may have little say in where the new house is

located. They can, on the other hand, arrange a mutual exchange with another tenant, but again the housing department, acting as a kind of 'gatekeeper', will make the final decision.

For those seeking to rent a house in the public sector for the first time, not only will they be subject to an *allocation policy*, but also to a *selection policy*. In some local authority areas this may be simply a matter of joining a waiting list and waiting their turn. In others, a points scheme is used where, in addition to waiting time, factors such as family size, or degree of overcrowding and ill-health, are taken into consideration. If large-scale slum clearance is taking place, families that have been on the housing waiting list for some time may be by-passed by those made homeless by demolition.

Other 'gatekeepers' affect potential movers in the private sector. These are landowners, developers, financial institutions and estate agents who channel particular groups into certain housing situations. Choice is often limited and competition may be intense.

Landowners obviously affect choice by the

extent to which they release land for residential development; *developers* exert a powerful influence by the types and numbers of houses they build in particular locations. *Financial institutions* have different policies which favour particular groups and penalise others. Building societies and banks in the UK, for example, favour young salaried employees, whose earnings are stable and where promotion is likely. A building society mortgage loan is usually between two-and-a-half and three times the borrower's annual income, so low-income workers have only limited purchasing power. Building societies also prefer to advance mortgages on relatively new property which is likely to be in the middle and outer suburbs. Major financing institutions may thus reinforce socio-economic segregation. In the USA where banks are important mortgage providers, the saying is that 'banks decide where people live'.

Estate agents may also wield enormous power in shaping the social geography of a city. This has been particularly significant where ethnic minority households wish to view property in neighbourhoods inhabited exclusively by members of the majority ethnic group. For example, a report of a United States Commission on Race and Housing in 1960 stated that the policy of real estate associations was that 'a realtor [a real estate agent] should never be instrumental in introducing into a neighbourhood a character of property or occupancy, members of any race or nationality, or any individual whose presence will clearly be detrimental to property values in that neighbourhood'. Among the contrivances used, according to one commentator, are quoting inflated prices, demanding excessive down-payments, saying the house is already sold, taking down 'For Sale' notices, and not keeping appointments. In the UK direct discrimination in housing was first made unlawful under the *1968 Race Relations Act*, but claims of discrimination still occur although most are never officially reported. In one recent year, 51 cases were reported to the Commission for Racial Equality and although 19 concerned private landlords and 11 concerned estate agents, 21 involved local authority departments.

Exercise 7.1

Residential mobility in Bristol

Study the table below and map opposite concerning the intra-urban movement of 50 households to owner-occupied houses in Westbury-on-Trym, a desirable residential area in Bristol.

a) Summarise the patterns and processes shown in the map and table.

a) Main reasons for moving to Westbury-on-Trym. *Source*: N. McBride, 1988.

Reason for moving	Not important Nos.	%	Important Nos.	%	Very important Nos.	%
To own a house	41	82	5	10	4	8
An increase in household size	33	66	8	16	9	18
A decrease in household size	41	82	4	8	5	10
Marriage	45	90	1	2	4	8
Retirement	46	92	3	6	1	2
Last dwelling too small	30	60	10	20	10	20
Last dwelling too large	40	80	5	10	5	10
Last dwelling too expensive	42	84	8	16	–	
Last dwelling too far from work	44	86	5	10	1	2
Last dwelling too far from friends/relatives	46	92	3	6	1	2
Unsavoury neighbours	47	94	3	6	–	
Promotion at work	42	84	5	10	3	6
Temporary arrangement	47	94	3	6	–	
Other	31	62	8	16	11	22

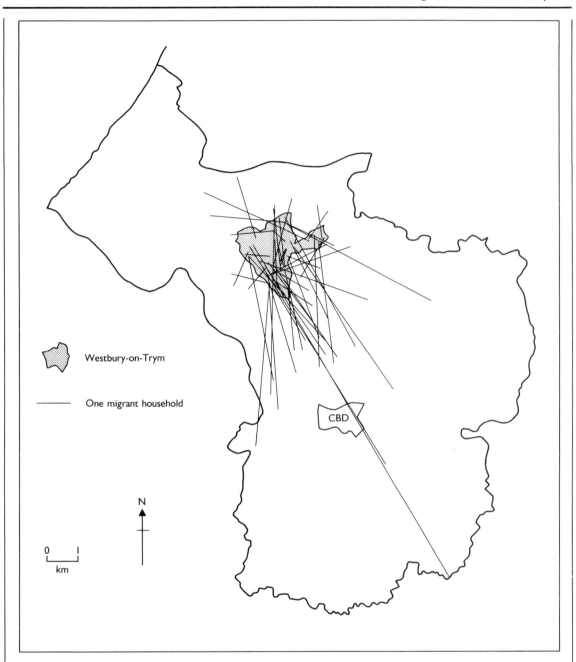

b) Direction and distance of movements of 50
households who moved to Westbury-on-Trym from
other parts of Bristol.
Source: N. McBride, 1988.

b) Discuss:
   i) The extent to which the map upholds the
      views put forward by John Adams
      concerning directional bias in intra-urban
      movements, and
   ii) the extent to which movements into
       Westbury-on-Trym are dominated by life-
       cycle reasons.

Residence and mobility in Third World cities

Interest in population mobility in Third World countries has focused largely on the massive rural–urban migrations that have been such a significant component of urban growth. These have clearly had a major influence on the numbers and kinds of people seeking accommodation in urban areas and thus on the housing market. Low-income groups form the vast majority of in-migrants to Third World cities, and Dwyer (1975) has attempted to summarise their movements in relation to different housing areas (Fig. 7.5).

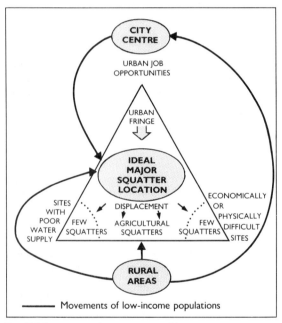

Fig. 7.5 Some typical movements of low-income populations to and in Third World cities.
Source: after Dwyer, 1975.

Early migrants mainly settled in the city centres where most employment opportunities were available. Once this pattern was established, later in-migrants often made contact with people from their own family or village already established in the city centre who might be able to help them find work or provide them with temporary accommodation. This is sometimes referred to as *chain migration*. Thus population continued to build up in the city centre and, as time went on, accommodation was often

Upper Nankin Street is in the heart of Singapore's 'Chinatown'. It is one of a grid of streets evidently laid out shortly after 1835. Apart from two vacant lots, it consists entirely of two- and three-storey shophouses built back-to-back to similar rows in the parallel streets. These shophouses, originally intended to house one or two families, have been subdivided by a maze of interior partitions into cubicles, the majority of which are without windows and in permanent semi-darkness. Most of these cubicles are about the size of two double beds, placed side by side. In one such cubicle – dark, confined, insanitary and without comfort – may live a family of seven or more persons. Many of them sleep on the floor, often under the bed. Their possessions are in boxes, placed on shelves to leave the floor free for sleeping. Their food is kept in tiny cupboards which hang from the rafters. Those who cannot even afford to rent a cubicle may live in a narrow bunk, often under the stairs. The number of cubicles varies considerably from one shophouse to another, from no. 13 with 24 cubicles and five spaces in addition to the shop on the ground floor (and a total of 83 residents!), to no. 25 with only six cubicles. The plan of a typical first floor is given here.

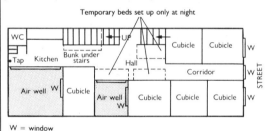

The tendency is for each first and second floor to have one kitchen, one bathroom and one toilet, regardless of the number of households. Ground floors are rarely provided with any of these facilities. Kitchens are mostly verandahs with the whole of one wall open to the sky and direct rain. The cooking is done for the most part in fire-buckets. Seventeen per cent of the floors surveyed are without a toilet; the average pressure on those on the remaining floors is 20 adults per toilet. All the toilets are of the open bucket type; only 36 per cent are emptied daily. When the buckets are emptied, they have to be carried through the kitchen and corridors, and down the stairs – inevitably some of the contents are spilled.

Fig. 7.6 Upper Nankin Street, Singapore, in the 1950s.
Source: after Kaye, 1960.

subdivided into smaller and smaller units. This process took place in central Singapore in the 1950s, and is graphically described by Kaye (1960) – Fig. 7.6.

As pressures on accommodation and services in the city centres increased, many people sought alternative accommodation outside the centre. The first to do so were usually members of elite groups who had traditionally occupied the central area but began to perceive other areas to be more attractive, as low-income groups moved into the centre and overcrowding increased. In some Latin American cities such as Bogotá and Quito, this kind of outward movement was occurring by the 1930s and has since been succeeded by further moves, often to sites even more distant from the centre. Each move has freed accommodation for groups of lower status, setting in train a process of filtering similar to that occasioned by the 'flight to the suburbs' of affluent city dwellers in many cities in the developed world. More recently, the growing affluence of particular groups in Asia and Africa has led to similar movements. In Nairobi, for example, the increased wealth of some Asian groups in Eastleigh (see Case Study 5B) led to their movement into better housing in Parklands and adjacent areas in the 1950s. They were largely replaced by upwardly mobile Africans moving from Eastlands into Eastleigh in what they, in turn, saw as a step up the socio-economic ladder.

As Fig. 7.5 indicates, however, low-income groups have often moved from city centres into areas of informal housing rather than being able to filter up the formal housing sector. In most Third World cities, housing provided within the 'formal' sector, built in accordance with official regulations, is far too expensive for most of the low-income population to buy or even rent. In these circumstances, people seeking cheaper or more spacious accommodation than they can obtain in the city centre, or perhaps wishing to be close to specific job opportunities in a peripheral area of the city, have moved into what have frequently been called 'squatter settlements'. This term, implying that settlers have no legal rights to the land they occupy, may not be strictly accurate and many other terms for this kind of settlement have been suggested, as will be discussed later. Whatever name they are given, however, settlements of this kind are an almost universal feature of Third World cities. Though often peripheral to a city, they may occupy previously unoccupied land anywhere within an urban area. Sites may be on land of poor quality

(for example steep slopes or ill-drained areas), on land left vacant for some reason (for example after demolition of earlier buildings) or where existing land uses do not preclude settlement construction (for example in cemeteries, as in Cairo's so-called 'City of the Dead'; alongside railway lines as in Delhi and Jakarta; or on municipal rubbish dumps as in Calcutta and Casablanca). Thus Dwyer's 'ideal major squatter location' (Fig. 7.5) could be in many different kinds of location but might be expected to provide proximity to employment, what are perceived as reasonable physical conditions for settlement, and available water supplies.

As the conventionally built-up area of the city expands, 'squatter settlements' may be displaced into less favourable sites in terms of physical conditions, water supply and proximity to jobs (Fig. 7.5). Rural–urban migrants will in some cases continue to move to city-centre accommodation but other migrants will move directly from the countryside or small towns to urban 'squatter settlements'. The nature of such settlements will change through time as a result both of individual and community actions. Housing may be of many different forms, ranging from primitive constructions of wood, polythene, mud bricks, scrap metal, bitumenised cardboard or any other materials the occupants can lay hands on, to quite well-built homes of brick or concrete. Evidence from many areas suggests that given some security of tenure or merely an absence of harassment by the authorities, improvements in housing and services are likely to occur through a process of self-help. The complexity of such settlements is thus considerable, offering a range of housing possibilities and creating difficulties, as suggested earlier, in devising appropriate terminology to describe them.

Although many early settlements of this kind were occupied by people with no legal rights to the land (squatters), this is often not the case today when, for example, landholdings have in some cases been legitimised in former squatter areas or land has been deliberately made available for housing low-income families. So-called 'sites and services' schemes are now widespread, with people being encouraged to build their homes on land provided by state or city authorities, with certain basic services such as water supplies and sewerage systems also

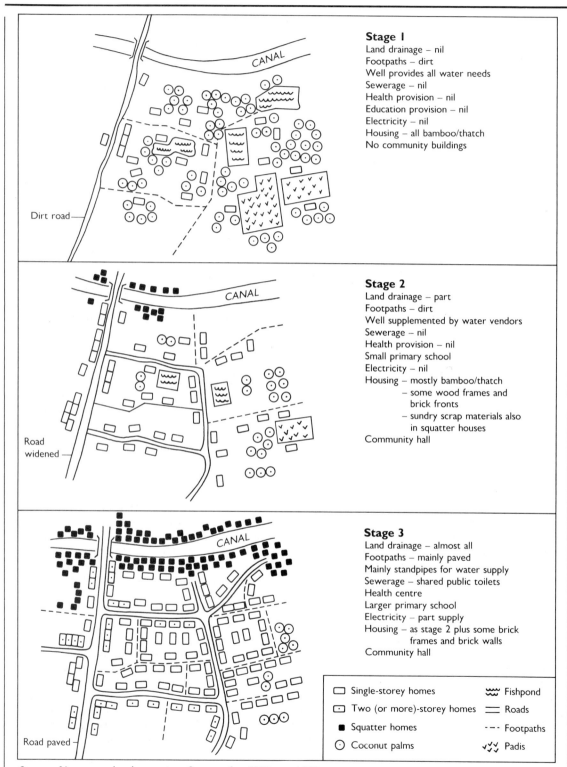

Stage 1
Land drainage – nil
Footpaths – dirt
Well provides all water needs
Sewerage – nil
Health provision – nil
Education provision – nil
Electricity – nil
Housing – all bamboo/thatch
No community buildings

Stage 2
Land drainage – part
Footpaths – dirt
Well supplemented by water vendors
Sewerage – nil
Health provision – nil
Small primary school
Electricity – nil
Housing – mostly bamboo/thatch
　　　　 – some wood frames and
　　　　　 brick fronts
　　　　 – sundry scrap materials also
　　　　　 in squatter houses
Community hall

Stage 3
Land drainage – almost all
Footpaths – mainly paved
Mainly standpipes for water supply
Sewerage – shared public toilets
Health centre
Larger primary school
Electricity – part supply
Housing – as stage 2 plus some brick
　　　　 frames and brick walls
Community hall

▭ Single-storey homes		〰 Fishpond
▱ Two (or more)-storey homes		═ Roads
■ Squatter homes		--- Footpaths
☉ Coconut palms		⩔⩔ Padis

Dirt road

Road widened

Road paved

Stages of kampung development.　*Source*: after Williams, 1975.

Exercise 7.2

Urban kampung development in Indonesia

In most large Indonesian cities, employment for many low-income migrants is provided by servicing the needs of richer city dwellers as rickshaw drivers, pedlars of food, drink and other consumer goods, domestic servants, labourers, etc. It is advantageous for those employed in this way to live as close as possible to their employment in housing provided by self-help construction or by renting as cheaply as possible. Often rural settlements (*kampungs*) adjacent to early urban centres have gradually been engulfed by city growth and have developed into much more densely settled 'urban *kampungs*' as rural–urban migrants have moved in. Legislation concerning land ownership is often unclear with no systematic land registration. In-migrants frequently pay former occupants for land on which to build their homes but they still have no legal right to the land. Squatting of a more normal kind may also occur. Since about 1970, government efforts to upgrade urban *kampungs* by improving roads, drainage and water supply and providing various community facilities have given residents a greater sense of security and encouraged private initiatives for improvement. These have often resulted in alterations to the socio-economic mix of *kampung* dwellers.

In the light of the above background information and the maps provided opposite, attempt the following:

a) Describe the main features of the *kampung* illustrated in stage 1, briefly suggesting reasons for the features shown.

b) Describe and suggest reasons for the physical changes shown to occur by stages 2 and 3, relating these both to the background information provided and to more general information about housing in Third World cities.

c) Suggest what patterns of 'filtering' might occur as the situation represented by the three stages develops, making reference both to movements of residents within the *kampung* and likely links to other typical housing areas.

d) Several Third World governments have tried to resolve urban housing problems by building high-rise blocks of flats rather than upgrading existing housing. What advantages and disadvantages might result from a policy of demolishing the *kampung* area shown and replacing it by high-rise housing?

being made available. Schemes of this kind are discussed further in Chapter 9. Although the term 'squatter settlement' is clearly not always appropriate, many other terms have also failed to find general favour including 'shanty towns' – one of the earlier descriptions – and 'spontaneous settlements' as suggested by Dwyer (1975). More recently, rather less specific terms have become common in attempts to describe the housing of the urban poor, though these again may be open to criticism. They include 'informal housing' (that is, housing not constructed as part of the formal, regulated building sector), 'self-help housing', 'uncontrolled housing' and 'unconventional housing'. Johnstone (1979, 1983) in his work on Malaysia defines unconventional housing as that which is built with little or no contact with modern institutions and which only occasionally meets established

building and planning regulations. Within that category he differentiates between *squatter housing*, where the housing occupies land without the landowner's permission, and *vernacular housing*, where this is not the case and where frequently the housing is of a type that is common in rural areas but does not comply with urban building regulations. Johnstone has suggested that in most Malaysian cities except Kuala Lumpur, vernacular housing is more extensive than squatter housing (Fig. 7.7). Local names for such unconventional or informal housing areas are even more numerous including the urban *kampungs* of Java, the *colonias proletarias* of Mexico, the *favelas* of Brazil and the graphically named *gecekondus* ('built by night') of Turkey and *callampas* ('mushrooms') of Chile.

The range of unconventional housing is

Fig. 7.7 Informal housing on the outskirts of Kuantan, a rapidly growing town on the east coast of Peninsular Malaysia. These homes fall into the category described by Johnstone as 'vernacular' housing. People living here are able to grow some crops as well as working in town. Rising living standards in Malaysia mean that many people can now afford to own a bicycle or motor-bike, and this makes it easier for them to live further from their place of work.

considerable in many Third World cities but, for any individual household, choice is constrained by such factors as capital available, income level, knowledge of opportunities and contacts with 'gatekeepers' who have accommodation to let or sell or who exercise control (though not necessarily legal rights) over land where housing may be built. Many low-income residents gradually improve their homes by self-help projects, re-building in better materials or adding extra rooms or facilities. As in developed countries, changes of residence often relate to stages of the family life-cycle such as marriage or the birth of a child. Many men work in urban areas for some years before their dependants move from rural areas to join them, possibly necessitating a change of residence for the man when his family join him. Quite often a man's wife and children never make the move to an urban home, however. This is a significant factor

influencing the failure to upgrade much unconventional housing in African cities.

Changing aspirations of individuals may also result in changes of residence. Turner (1968), largely on the basis of Latin American experience, differentiated between the following groups, each with different priorities:

1 *Very low-income bridgeheaders* – new migrants whose main concern is to find any accommodation they can afford as close as possible to potential sources of employment.
2 *Low-income consolidators* – more established in the city and concerned to live in rather better housing even if this is further from their place of work.
3 *Middle-income status seekers* – who have achieved economic security and so are likely to move to areas within the city that will provide them with the social status they now desire.

Clearly not all low-income migrants to the city move through a sequence represented by these three groupings (for example most of those whose wives remain in rural areas), but the aspirations implicit in the different categories do suggest some reasons for intra-urban movements.

Another major influence on movements of low-income urban residents in the Third World is the attitude of the urban authorities. The importance of granting legal rights to land is clearly significant in providing security of tenure. Where such rights are not granted and official harassment occurs then settlements may be destroyed, and forced migration of the inhabitants may occur. Forced migration may also result from the destruction of unconventional settlements when the authorities are genuinely trying to improve living conditions by offering alternative accommodation, as in the public housing schemes of Singapore and Hong Kong.

While some features of housing provision for and residential mobility of low-income groups in Third World cities are fairly common, there are many differences in detail between cities and often considerable complexity within them.

A small-scale study of residential mobility in Sheffield

This analysis of residential mobility in the owner-occupied sector in two neighbourhoods in the city of Sheffield is a summary of part of a larger study carried out in 1988–89 (Mason, 1989). It highlights a number of generalisations discussed in the first half of the chapter and illustrates the need to take into account the unique geography of any place in understanding spatial processes.

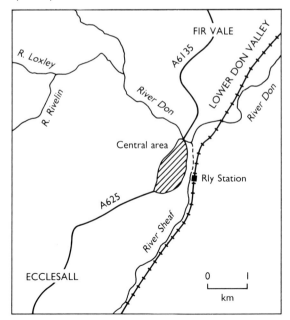

Fig. 7.8 The location of Fir Vale and Ecclesall.

The two neighbourhoods are Fir Vale and Ecclesall, whose locations are shown in Fig. 7.8. Fir Vale is an area of relatively low-priced terrace houses built about 90–100 years ago, lying some 5 km to the north-east of the city centre. Gardens are non-existent or very small and cars have to be parked on the street. Many residents of the area claim some form of state welfare and a substantial proportion belong to ethnic minority groups. Ecclesall is in complete contrast to Fir Vale. It is an exclusive residential area about 4 km to the south-west of the city centre astride a major road leading towards the Peak District. Houses are in a variety of styles ranging from traditional suburban detached and semi-detached homes to mock Tudor villas and ranch-style bungalows, all set on wide, tree-lined streets, avenues and closes. All have garages and substantial gardens.

Fifty owner-occupiers in each area who had moved to their present address from elsewhere in Sheffield (inter-urban migrants were excluded) were questioned about where they had moved from and the principal reasons for their move. Of the 50 heads of household interviewed in *Fir Vale*, 26 were in manual employment, 1 was in a professional occupation, 11 were unemployed and 12 were retired. The dominant reason given – 13 cases – for moving to their present address was marriage. Five moves were prompted by the need to find a larger house, and four (all retired households) had moved into a smaller property. Eleven respondents gave the desire to own a home as the major reason for moving. These were from households who had previously been in council accommodation or living with parents. Eight of the moves were involuntary, mostly the result of urban renewal schemes. Two respondents had moved to be nearer a new place of work. The remaining seven respondents could not offer one dominant reason for their move. When asked about their previous address it was found that 45 of the 50 Fir Vale respondents had moved less than 5 km, with just over two-thirds moving less than 1 km. Only eight of the moves were in an outward direction from the city centre, in contradiction to Adams' directional bias hypothesis, although most moves originated in the north-eastern quadrant of the city, supporting his sector hypothesis. Only three of the 50 households had crossed the CBD to their present home.

Most of the 50 heads of household in *Ecclesall* were middle-aged or elderly (only 14 were under the age of 44). Twelve were retired and 34 of the remaining 38 were in professional occupations. Twenty-two of the 50 respondents said they had moved to their present address principally for more space, and eight had moved to a smaller house. Only six gave marriage as their main motivation for moving – not surprising in view of the high house prices in the area. The remaining 14 respondents gave a variety of reasons for the move to their present address, including divorce, separation and widowhood (four cases) and change of job (two cases). As in Fir Vale, moves were over relatively short distances – 43 of the 50 were less than 5 km and 22 were less than 3 km. However, only a minority of moves –16 – were in an outward direction from the city centre. Only two moves had originated north of the CBD.

Despite major differences in the location and character of the two areas and the socio-economic characteristics of the sample population, the patterns and processes of residential mobility are very similar. In both areas the single most important reason for moving was what can be termed a 'life-cycle' reason: an event such as marriage, the loss of a partner through separation, divorce or death, the need for more space when a family grows and the desire for a smaller house when children grow up and move away. Such considerations accounted for 22 of the moves in Fir Vale and 40 in Ecclesall. The study also underlines the fact that job changes, such as change of career or promotion or transfer, though of overwhelming importance in inter-urban moves are of little importance at the intra-urban scale, with only four out of the 100 intra-urban moves being principally prompted by such considerations.

Finally, although the vast majority of moves in the two areas were principally from one quadrant of the city – the north-east quadrant in the case of Fir Vale and the south-west quadrant in the case of Ecclesall – with little crossing of the CBD, Adams' narrowly sectoral outward movement hypothesis is not substantiated. In both areas there was at least as much lateral and inward movement as outward movement. In the case of Ecclesall, the majority of moves from outside the area originated in high-status areas in other parts of the city, often further from the centre. In the case of Fir Vale, the complex pattern of movements from all directions but from a fairly restricted area can be partly explained by the presence of members of ethnic minority groups moving within a relatively restricted area, and by former council tenants moving from estates to the south-east and north-east.

8

The economic geography of urban areas

Urban areas are locations of intense economic activity in manufacturing, retailing, financial and legal services and other types of office employment, and in personal services such as hotel accommodation and entertainment. In the countries of the developed world during the 100 years from the middle of the 19th century, manufacturing congregated increasingly in extensive industrial districts, and retailing, office employment and personal services became overwhelmingly concentrated in the central commercial area. The last 40 years or so have seen dramatic changes in these spatial patterns resulting from changing economic, political, social and technological circumstances. Changes in Third World cities have been more recent and in some ways less dramatic but nevertheless considerable.

Land values and spatial patterns of economic activity

Traditionally the location of economic activities in the city has been seen in terms of the bid-rent model (Fig. 8.1) which shows the rent-paying abilities of different types of activities. In the diagram it is assumed that the city centre is the most accessible and thus the most sought-after location. Rents will therefore be highest there and will decline with distance from the centre. This gives rise to a more or less concentric pattern of land use in which shops and offices concentrate at the centre, with light manufacturing and warehousing forming a middle ring and residences forming a broad outer ring. Specialised industrial districts along waterfronts or railways may cut across these concentric zones to some extent.

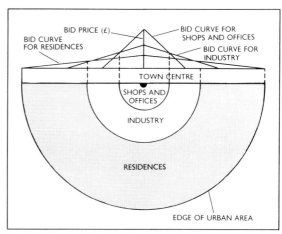

Fig. 8.1 The traditional bid-rent model.

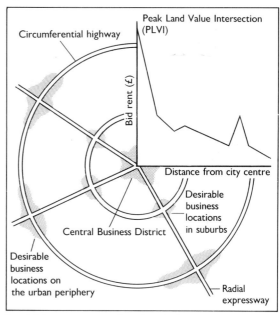

Fig. 8.2 Incorporation of modern highway developments to produce a more realistic land value 'surface'.

The traditional bid-rent model may be criticised on a number of grounds. One weakness is that it disregards the fact that in the second half of the 20th century, urban areas may consist not just of one nucleus but of a number of nuclei, as a result of the creation of new towns on the periphery of urban areas and the engulfment of once-independent communities. It also does not take account of rising affluence and associated transport developments. More and more families own cars and this allows much more flexibility in journeys to work and to the shops. It may also result in increased congestion in the central area. Development of urban motorways, both radial and circumferential, to cater for increased private and commercial road vehicles, may also create desirable industrial and commercial as well as residential locations outside the central area. A more realistic land value 'surface' may look like that portrayed in Fig. 8.2 but these new locations will be viewed differently by the various business enterprises operating within any one city.

Retailing activity

The best-known classification of retailing activity in the city is Berry's 1963 classification based on a study of Chicago. It includes three basic types: centres, ribbons and specialised areas (Fig. 8.3). The *centres* form a well-defined hierarchy from the isolated convenience store at the bottom to the central business district (CBD) at the top. Each step in the hierarchy is marked by increased size of centre in terms of outlets and functions and by increased size of trade area. Retail *ribbons* are conspicuous features of American cities and may take a number of different forms.

The traditional shopping street is simply a linear type of neighbourhood shopping centre which caters for passing traffic as well as the local population. Urban arterial ribbons contain businesses requiring access to a city-wide clientele but which use considerable amounts of space, such as DIY centres and car-repair shops. New suburban ribbons and highway-oriented ribbons are not easily differentiated: both contain restaurants, car-repair stations, cocktail lounges and ice-cream parlours. The highway-oriented ribbons cater for inter-urban clientele rather than local customers, and so motels are an important additional activity. The *specialised areas* are largely self-explanatory. Those most familiar to Europeans are entertainments districts (for example Soho or Shaftesbury Avenue in London), and markets.

The American classification is not directly applicable to areas outside North America but many similarities exist. For example, in a study of Coventry it was found that both centres (called *nucleations*) and ribbons could be identified. The ribbons in Coventry were found predominantly in the inner city and were outgrowths of former nucleations. The absence

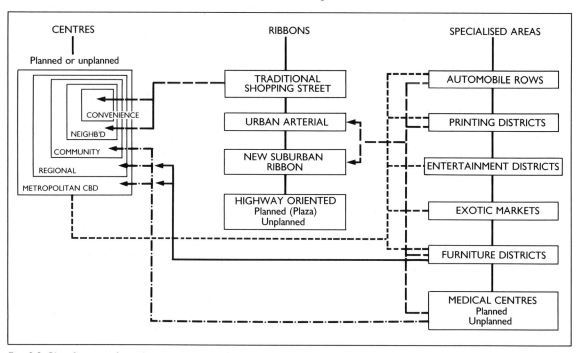

Fig. 8.3 Classification of retailing activity in an American city.
Source: Berry, 1963.

of outer city ribbons of the highway-oriented type reflects lower levels of car ownership and the much stricter imposition of planning regulations in the UK compared with the USA. Another interesting feature of the study was that the size groupings of the nucleations showed a much more obvious hierarchical structure (as in the Chicago study) than was the case when nucleations, ribbons and mixed types were ranked together.

Retailing changes in the developed world

An important development in retailing in the cities of the developed world, particularly in the last 40 years, is the growth of new types of retail outlet in the outer parts of cities and beyond the city boundaries in smaller communities. This happened first in North America in response to rapid decentralisation of populations and high levels of car ownership. Three types of new centre, in terms of size and form, have appeared in North American suburbs: regional, community and neighbourhood centres. These are the planned centres in Berry's classification (Fig. 8.3), but they are planned only in the sense that they have been developed as integrated units by a developer; they are not built by local planning authorities. The largest type, the regional centres, of which there are more than 400 in the USA and Canada, occupy at least 40,000 m^2 and have parking space for about 4,000 cars. Their catchment areas may contain as many as 250,000 people. They have at least one major department store and numerous speciality shops, as well as restaurants and supermarkets. They are often located at the junction of circumferential and radial highways (see Fig. 8.2), sometimes as far as 20–30 km from the CBD. They are often designed on the 'mall' plan with speciality shops facing each other across covered, air-conditioned pedestrian walkways with department stores at each end.

Planned surburban shopping centres of the American type are also found in Canada, Australia, Japan and most parts of north-west Europe. In Britain, with its tight planning controls on commercial development and restricted suburban sprawl, centres of the size of the American regional types are still relatively uncommon, although neighbourhood-type centres are found in new residential neighbour-

hoods. Brent Cross Centre in north-west London was the first development in this country to compare with an American regional centre in terms of size and layout. It occupies 90,000 m^2, has parking spaces for 4,500 cars, and there are 1.25 million potential customers within 20–25 minutes' car driving time. It contains two department stores (John Lewis and Fenwick), four multiple stores (including a Marks and Spencer store) and 90 smaller units mainly occupied by jewellery, shoe and fashion shops. It has since been followed by the Metro Centre on Tyneside, Merry Hill in the West Midlands (Case Study 8A), and a number of others.

One type of suburban shopping centre that has seen remarkable growth in the UK in recent years is the *superstore*. A superstore has at least 2,500 m^2 of sales area and comprises a one-storey, 'one-stop' shopping centre carrying a wide range of food and non-food lines including items for gardening, clothes, car accessories and DIY. Sales are by self-service and payment is made at a series of checkouts. Additionally there may be a cafeteria, a petrol station and a small number of other specialist outlets. A ground-level car park is provided adjacent to the store. In France the term *hypermarket* (*hypermarché*) is used for units over 2,500 m^2 (in the UK the term 'hypermarket' is reserved for superstores over 5,000 m^2), and by 1984 there were just over 500 such stores in France. In the UK there were 300 superstores and hypermarkets in the mid-1980s. In the UK much controversy surrounds the development of free-standing hypermarkets and regional centres located on the urban periphery, on the grounds that they may lead to the decline of existing shopping centres and that they discriminate against less affluent, car-less households.

Obviously, the rapid retailing developments on the edges of urbanised areas in developed world cities were bound to have repercussions in the older inner urban centres and in the central commercial area. There has been decline and attempts to arrest decline, particularly through re-development schemes. In North America, in spite of these schemes, the central shopping area has declined in importance and at the same time its role has changed somewhat. Whereas before 1945 it supplied 'mass appeal' and specialised goods for the whole of the urban area, it now provides mass-appeal goods (for example food, furniture, clothes) only for inner-city residents, for visitors and for those who work in the central areas. For those Americans and Canadians who live and, increasingly, work in the suburbs, the dominance of the central shopping area is a thing of the past.

In Western Europe, there is much stronger attachment to the central area for historical reasons. Suburbanisation occurred at a later date than in North America and local authorities invested much capital in rebuilding city centres after the Second World War and have since sought to protect their investments by turning down many applications for suburban retailing

Exercise 8.1

Surburban retailing

A recent analysis of large suburban shopping centres in a provincial English city identified *four* main types:

1 *Large district centres* These have a wide variety of goods in a large number of shop units. Each contains a superstore or more than one large supermarket and a number of other food shops. They also include a whole range of retail and complementary non-retail functions. They are located some distance from the city centre, but they are not 'out in the suburbs'. Most are *nodal* in form. Being on major transport routes they suffer serious congestion problems. They contain recent major shopping developments, and vacancy rates are low. They are thriving centres.

2 *Food-oriented district centres* These centres have fewer units than type 1 and are oriented towards food shopping. They usually contain medium-sized supermarkets and a range of other food shops. Other types of shops, for example those selling household goods, are under-represented. Most of these centres are in the older parts of the city, but are a reasonable distance away from the city centre. Some are *nodal* and some are *linear*. Some of these centres are thriving but others are in decline, reflected in their high vacancy rates and shabby and unattractive appearance.

3 *Specialist shopping centres* These centres are all on radial routes stretching outwards from the city centre and are therefore *linear*. Their specialisations vary: some specialise in catering – wine-bars, restaurants and take-aways – others specialise in food-retailing for ethnic minorities, one is a second-hand furniture/ antiques centre, and two others specialise in clothes and shoes. For these specialised functions the centres serve a wide area but they all have a local role and some contain large or medium-sized supermarkets. These centres also vary a great deal in their prosperity. Some are upmarket and thriving; others are in decline and contain a substantial number of vacant units.

4 *Superstore-dominated district centres* There was only one centre in this category. Although it contained a small street market which operated two days a week, and a number of other shops, it was dominated by an Asda superstore. Because of the dominance of Asda, there were few other shops selling food and a substantial number of units were non-retail, for example catering establishments, building society branches and banks. This centre was on the urban periphery where there has been much recent residential development near a motorway intersection and a suburban railway station.

a) Summarise the analysis in cartographic form.

b) Suggest why some shopping centres of type 2 face stagnation and decline.

c) Make a field-based study of a suburban shopping centre, paying particular attention to its location, its form, the range and proportions of goods sold, any significant non-retail functions, degree of specialisation, store sizes and types (for example independents, local, regional or national chains, over-the-counter service, self-service supermarkets, superstore, etc.), vacancy rates, physical condition of individual shops and the centre as a whole, including litter and vandalism, and parking provision.

d) Place your selected centre, with a reasoned justification, within the typology 1–4 provided above. If it does not fit easily into any of the four categories, make out a case for identifying an additional type.

development. Consequently the central shopping areas in Western Europe are much more dominant in the total retailing system than in North America. Nevertheless they have been subject to much change. Two of the most significant changes are the creation of pedestrian precincts and the development of central area shopping centres of the mall type. Pedestrianised streets, with the addition of new pavement surfaces, seats and shrubbery, are a familiar feature of most British towns, large and small, and are characteristic of many cities in other European countries. New covered shopping centres are particularly marked features of central area redevelopment schemes in Britain, where they constitute joint ventures between local planning authorities and private developers. They differ from North American suburban planned centres in that they are often multi-storey (shopping units and parking spaces) and irregular in shape, contain a greater variety of shops, and are often adjacent to public transport termini (Fig. 8.4).

Fig. 8.4 The Ridings shopping centre, Wakefield, West Yorkshire. This is a typical town-centre 'mall type' development. It is multi-storey, with roof-top car parking, and is adjacent to the central bus station. It has attracted a wide variety of high street multiples.

In Eastern Europe there have been suburban developments of a different kind in the last 35 years. As a result of population expansion and the need to rebuild after the destruction of the Second World War, much residential development has been in the form of new neighbourhoods, often in the form of groups of tower blocks. Retail services are present in each neighbourhood but only rarely are they in shopping precincts or centres. They are usually dispersed, at ground-floor level, within the residential blocks. In cases of laundries and dry-cleaners they are often in basements. A good deal of walking, therefore, may be required for everyday convenience shopping.

Retailing in the Third World

Not dissimilar developments have occurred in some Third World cities with the development of high-rise housing schemes away from the city centre, for example in Singapore. Such developments are accompanied by considerable commercial developments to provide for the everyday needs of the local population. There have been new town, in-town developments of a similar kind in Latin America in some of the largest cities such as Caracas, Mexico City and São Paulo. These new towns within the city boundaries but outside the central area, like the Singapore housing estates, include industrial, commercial and other facilities as well as housing areas.

It is not easy to generalise about Third World urban retailing patterns, however, for individual cities reflect a mixture of indigenous retailing patterns, Westernised developments and often also patterns related to other immigrant communities, for example the 'Chinatowns' of many South-East Asian cities. The wealthy minority in such cities have a strong influence on new developments (see earlier comments on the 'spine' of large Latin American cities in Chapter 5), and a marked duality in retail provision is still apparent in many cities, with the poorer elements still dependent largely on traditional outlets, street vendors and sometimes municipal markets. Changes are occurring, however, and it is interesting to note the varying success of attempts to develop municipal markets (*galeria*) in the Colombian town of Cali outside the city centre where problems have been encountered because of competition from supermarkets offering a wider range of merchandise, more convenient shopping facilities and a more modern 'image'.

Office activity

In the traditional bid-rent model (see Fig. 8.1), offices, like specialist shops, are shown to be concentrated in the central area, but like retailing, certain types of offices have decentralised. Certain office activities have long been located in suburban areas in developed countries, for example branch banks, travel agents and estate agents. Others such as stockbrokers, investment companies and merchant bankers, dependent upon frequent face-to-face contact with one another, with government officials and with their professional advisers (for example accountancy and advertising firms) have long been concentrated in the central area and appear likely to continue to be in the foreseeable future. Other types of office activity which have also congregated traditionally in the centre are company headquarters and insurance companies. In these cases, prestige and accessibility for large clerical and middle management workforces have been important reasons for their central locations. It is the presence of all these types of office activity on expensive land that has given the CBD its characteristic skyline, at first in North America and more recently in the rest of the world's largest cities, including those of the Third World. Figure 8.5, showing the CBD of Toronto, Canada, clearly illustrates the visual impact of the central location of office activities.

Decentralisation of office activity has been taking place in North America for some time, and more recently in the rest of the developed world. The reasons for this are varied. In the USA the movement of millions of Americans into new and expanding suburban communities outside the main cities has meant that peripheral locations are more appropriate in terms of worker accessibility. Increased congestion in the central area and the shortage and cost of parking facilities are also powerful contributory factors. Lower rates, room for expansion and opportunities for developing landscaped sites are added attractions of suburban locations. Another advantage in many cities is greater accessibility to a major airport. Outside North America the same push and pull factors are prising offices from central locations, with the addition, in some countries, of government pressure. In Paris, for example, firms developing new office space in the CBD are charged a 'congestion tax' and in London, between 1963 and 1977, the Location of Offices Bureau (LOB) assisted in the relocation of 150,000 office jobs from the central area to other parts of the metropolitan region and the rest of the country. Decentralisation of office activity is less common in Third World cities but is already apparent in some of the large cities such as Bogotá, Cairo and Hong Kong.

In the USA and Canada, office decentralisation has been strongly linked with the development of *office parks*. Here a number of office buildings are brought together on a landscaped site, usually close to a high-status residential area, with good access to a major airport and often including a shopping centre and recreational facilities. Large numbers of such parks now encircle the major regional capitals in the USA (Fig. 8.6). Office parks are less common outside North America. One of the largest in Western Europe is the City-Nord project, 6 km north of the centre of Hamburg in Germany.

Fig. 8.5 Central business district, Toronto, Canada. With a population of more than 2 million, Toronto is the business and English-speaking cultural 'capital' of Canada. It has major banking and publishing functions and its stock exchange is one of the most important in North America. Much of the 'downtown' area has been re-built in the last 20 years. The photograph was taken from the CN Tower, the highest free-standing structure in the world.

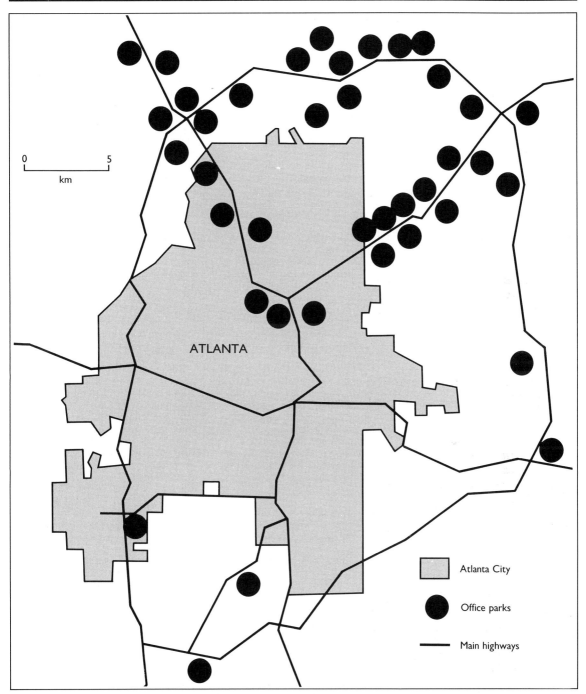

Fig. 8.6 Office parks in the Atlanta metropolitan area in the early 1970s. It should be noted that all but 7 of the 39 office parks were outside Atlanta City, in neighbouring suburban communities. Note the attraction of the modern highways for such developments.
Source: after Association of American Geographers, 1973.

Exercise 8.2

Head office relocation from London

Read the press cutting below.

Head Offices on the Move

FOR COMMUTERS travelling by car into central London, the journey to work can be a nightmare. But not for the chairman and chief executive of IBM UK. While most managing directors of major companies are threading their way slowly through congested streets, IBM UK's chief is speeding through the Hampshire countryside to an office from which he can hear the plaintive cry of seabirds rather than the roar of city traffic.

In the early 1970s, wanting room to expand, IBM UK moved their head office from London to Portsmouth. Other firms made similar moves: Burmah Oil went to Swindon, Metal Box to Reading, Wiggins Teape to Basingstoke.

The reasons for moving were varied. Burmah Oil, like IBM UK, wanted more room for expansion. Wiggins Teape occupied a high-value, much sought-after site in the City near St Paul's, so would profit financially from the move. The chairman of Metal Box wanted a better working and living environment for his staff. By the beginning of the 1970s London was becoming an increasingly difficult place in which to work: in particular, there were long, uncomfortable and expensive journeys to work, cramped working conditions, and high house prices. But there was opposition from some senior company figures to the proposed moves. Could the head offices of major companies, they asked, operate efficiently outside London, away from the City, Whitehall, Fleet Street and the Inns of Court?

The evidence now seems to suggest that they can. NatWest, IBM UK's banker, improved its foreign business facilities in Portsmouth and hired specialist staff. Barclays did much the same for Burmah at Swindon. A local firm of accountants in Portsmouth were found by IBM to be every bit as good as its London counterpart.

The need to be in the City of London is now seen by many as a myth. But the decentralisation of headquarters offices has meant longer days for top executives. London meetings are still frequent and more careful planning of the working day and working week are necessary. London meetings have to be grouped together rather than spread out over the week. The car phone is now a necessity: the car is a mobile office.

The greatest advantage of a head office located outside London is reduced costs. Metal Box had a £19m profit from the move to Reading; IBM, which did not own their London office, gained through lower rents and rates.

There is also the benefit, in many cases, of a purpose-built headquarters building. Metal Box included squash courts and an indoor heated swimming pool in their new Reading headquarters. IBM designed their new headquarters with expansion in mind – not something that could have been contemplated in London, on the grounds of cost and available space.

Another bonus is lower staff losses. Metal Box have reported that they are keeping people very much longer than they did in London. This means they spend less on training and therefore achieve a higher level of productivity. At Portsmouth, IBM's staff turnover is 50 per cent lower than it was in London. With no London allowance to pay, the wage bill has also decreased.

But there are problems involved in leaving London. The extra travelling involved for senior staff adds to job stress. Recruiting specialists can also be a problem – tax lawyers and business analysts may feel cut off outside London. They may miss day-to-day contacts with others in the same field and also miss what is called the 'City adrenalin'. There is sometimes the feeling that the business cutting edge is being blunted in the 'small town' environments to which firms have moved.

The receiving towns have embraced the newcomers whole-heartedly. The new firms have contributed handsomely to the rates and helped to provide civic amenities. Shops and restaurants have benefited and, above all, jobs have been created.

a) What are the attractions of a City of London location for the head office of a large company?

b) What are the disadvantages of such a location?

c) Argue the case *for* and *against* a large firm moving its head office from London to a medium-sized town outside the capital.

d) It is noticeable that all the receiving towns mentioned in the article are in southern England. A large firm is less likely to move its headquarters from London to a town in the north of England, Wales or Scotland. Why do you think this is so?

In Britain one of the earliest developments of this type is the Aztec West office park on the outskirts of Bristol. It is situated near the junction of the M4 and M5 motorways north of Bristol, and when work began on it in the early 1980s it was the first true greenfield office park on the American model in this country. It will eventually comprise about 186,000 m² of warehouse, office and industrial space on a landscaped site of 70 hectares arranged in a campus-style development incorporating shops, banks and leisure facilities. The aim is to create a village-centre atmosphere.

The office park concept is also being used to revitalise inner-city sites. For example, it is being used to revive Trafford Park in Manchester, Britain's largest industrial estate which employs 27,000 people but which has been in decline for decades. Between now and the end of the century it is planned to develop 450,000 m² of land in a new 'Wharfside' project around the little used and shabby upper reaches of the Manchester Ship Canal (Fig. 8.7). The development, which is only 1.5 km from Manchester city centre and 14 km from Manchester airport, is planned to

include office, industrial, retail, leisure, hotel and car parking space. The projected office development will be in a lake and parkland setting with a promenade along the frontage of the Ship Canal. The scheme also includes improved links to the nearby motorway network and a rapid transit system. If all the Wharfside project plans come to fruition, this development, together with a similar one already virtually complete to the north at Salford Quays, will transform the office employment patterns and the land value surface of the inner part of Greater Manchester.

Manufacturing

Like retailing and office activity, manufacturing has been subject to decentralisation in the last 30 years, yet in most major cities, industrial districts which originated in the 19th century or even earlier contain a substantial amount of all manufacturing activity. Although the industrial geography of any city is unique, as a result of its site characteristics and historical accidents, it is

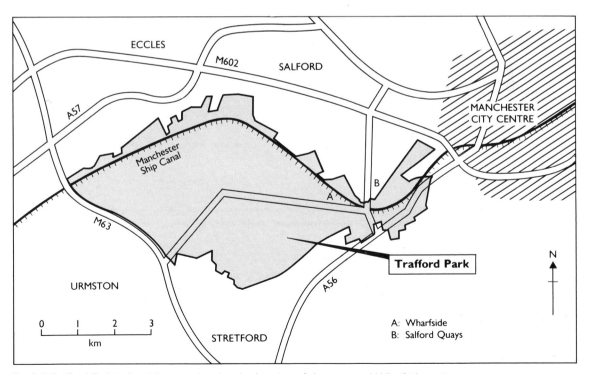

Fig. 8.7 Trafford Park industrial estate showing the location of the proposed Wharfside project.

Fig. 8.8 Urban manufacturing locations in a city in the developed world. (See the text for an explanation.)

possible to generalise about urban manufacturing locations (Fig. 8.8).

Type A industries are found in the CBD. In most cities only printing and publishing are in this category, and in the largest cities give rise to specialised districts such as the now rapidly declining Fleet Street in London.

Outside the CBD in cities in the developed world there is usually a discontinuous mixed zone of manufacturing, warehouses and residences. Two types of industry may be found here. *Type B1* industries, such as brewing and baking, are those that are found in all cities and which serve a city-wide market including the central commercial zone. *Type B2* industries are those that have evolved from light craft industries, and the origins of the districts they now occupy may go back to the old craft quarters of the pre-industrial town. This is true, for example, of the inner-city cutlery quarters in Sheffield, and the clothing districts of the East End of London. Such industries are often characterised by complex local industrial linkages so that in a clothing quarter, zip manufacturers and button makers are in close attendance.

Heavy industrial districts contain *type C* industries. These are usually large-scale industries that originated mostly, but not exclusively, more than 50 years ago. Some of them use bulky materials brought from other regions or from overseas. Much land is used for storage of raw materials and products awaiting dispatch. The industrial districts in which they lie may have developed on an ocean or lake waterfront, along a navigable waterway or on an important railway route. Industries in this category include oil refining, heavy chemicals, steelmaking, heavy engineering, flour milling, sugar refining and some types of textile production.

Type D industries are those that have no particular locational preferences and which may be found near the central area, on the urban periphery and in many other parts of the urban area. They are usually in small- to medium-sized plants and their location may be as much to do with the availability of suitable premises as with locational advantages. Light engineering and electronics are typical of these groups of industries.

Type E industries, which locate on the urban periphery and beyond, include all types of industry, even the very heaviest, if the urban periphery and estuary or coast happen to coincide, as they do at for example the Llanwern steelworks on the edge of Newport in South Wales. Peripherally located industries include modern industries whose only location has been suburban, and relocated industries from inner-city areas and old industrial districts. Among the factors encouraging the abandonment of inner-city sites are increased congestion, lack of room for expansion, obsolescent plant unsuitable for automated production, lack of storage and loading facilities, and re-development schemes which have given precedence to non-industrial land uses. At the same time, improved road networks in the suburbs, room for specialised layouts and later expansion, lower rates and rents and, in some cases, government grants have all encouraged the suburbanisation of manufacturing.

One characteristic shared by many industries at or beyond the urban periphery is their location on *industrial estates*, or 'industrial parks' as they are known in North America. An industrial estate is a group of industrial establishments provided with certain services and facilities laid down in advance. A variation on the industrial park is the *science park* which caters for high-technology industry and research and development departments of large firms. These parks are usually located near universities to take advantage of related research projects, scientific expertise and computing facilities. There are more than 50 such parks in the USA, but fewer than 10 in the UK.

Industrial estates have helped to provide industrial growth in many Third World cities where previously industrial development was limited. Many such estates have been developed since the 1940s, frequently sited on or beyond the urban periphery but also sometimes on other areas of previously open space within the city. One of the most successful has been the Jurong Industrial Estate in Singapore to which many foreign and local firms have been attracted by tax concessions, a hard-working and increasingly skilful labour force, and a lack of government 'red tape'. In 1960 the area that is now occupied by this estate consisted largely of swamp and small islands. Twenty years later over 1,000 companies employed nearly 100,000 workers on the estate – a remarkable development by any standards. A major advantage of industrial estates in developing countries is their provision of services which may not be easily available elsewhere – such items as electricity, water supplies and good road access. In many cases the initial provision of services and often the management of the estates is in the hands of local, regional or national government organisations, and estates have played an important part in promoting economic growth in several countries, for example Malaysia and South Korea, though there is often a tendency for estates in the largest towns to be more successful than those in smaller urban settlements in terms of attracting investors.

'Informal' economic activities in Third World cities

One of the main economic contrasts between cities in developed and less developed countries relates to the limited provision in the latter of employment of a conventional 'Western' type. The difficulties of providing adequate employment opportunities have resulted in the evolution of economic structures that are in some ways very different from those of the more developed countries, though it would be misleading to imply that some aspects are not also very similar. For example, the central areas of Third World cities provide a range of employment in retailing, offices and light industries similar in kind, if not always in quantity, to that of Western cities and, as already suggested, industrial estates in less developed countries are comparable in many ways to those in other parts of the world.

Overall, however, the development of conventional Western economic activities in general and of industry in particular has been limited in Third World cities. One reason for this has been the practice of colonial powers to restrict industrial development in colonial cities to relatively simple activities, mainly involving the processing of primary produce. Since independence, such factors as the limited home markets for industrial goods, the difficulties of competing in foreign markets, the shortage of capital for investment and, in some cases, limited managerial and entrepreneurial skills and experience have tended to reinforce the pre-independence situation in many countries.

With this background, a situation has developed where two main kinds of economic activity and organisation exist alongside each other. The first of these is basically similar to those of most cities in developed countries, the second very different. They have been variously described as 'firm-centred' and 'bazaar' economies (Geertz, 1963), 'formal' and 'informal' sectors (ILO, 1972), and 'upper' and 'lower' circuits (Santos, 1979). Figure 8.9 is an attempt to characterise the two 'sectors' or 'circuits' of the economy. This division into two neatly separated groups has been criticised as mislead-

Characteristics	Formal	Informal
Ownership	Corporate ownership	Usually family ownership
Technology	Capital-intensive	Labour-intensive
Capital	Relatively abundant	Scarce
Skills	Often acquired within formal education/training	Usually acquired outside formal education system
Hours of work	Regular system	Irregular
Scale of operation	Large (unless very high-quality product)	Small
Prices	Generally fixed	Usually negotiable (by haggling)
Credit source	Banks and other formal institutions	Personal, non-institutional sources
Profit margins	Often small per unit but large turnover	Often large per unit but small turnover
Relations with customers	Impersonal and often on paper	Direct and personal
Fixed costs	Substantial	Limited
Publicity	Large-scale and necessary	Usually none except personal recommendation
Re-use of good	None; gives rise to waste products	Frequent
Government aid	Extensive in many cases	Rare and very limited in quantity
Direct dependence on foreign countries	Considerable: essential to many firms	Little or none

Fig. 8.9 Some general characteristics of the 'formal' and 'informal' sectors of the economy.

ing and the concept of a continuum of economic activities ranging from clearly 'formal' to very 'informal' extremes has been suggested as an alternative. Without doubt there is much inter-linking and interaction between different types of economic activity which can result in problems of classification. Many street traders, normally seen as participating in the informal sector, sell products manufactured in the formal sector, for example. The construction of homes for the urban poor is often a result of both 'informal' and 'formal' activities, where, for example, the formal sector may provide some building materials and the informal sector other materials and 'self-help' labour. Despite difficulties of classification, the two-sector concept provides a useful working model. It is considerably more misleading to think of the formal sector as the realm of 'modern' activities and the informal sector as 'traditional'. Although

some activities in the informal sector are based on traditional rural skills (for example the brewing of beer), many are not, and most are a result of the process of modernisation which has brought about large-scale urbanisation and the demand for the products of the informal sector which principally serves the urban poor. Many activities also depend on by-products or waste materials from the formal sector which did not even exist in 'traditional' times, for example the production of sandals from old car tyres or the manufacture of many items from oil cans bought or scavenged in their hundreds from garages. Even the vast numbers of Third World city dwellers who make a living by re-processing or distributing items reclaimed from municipal rubbish dumps (see Case Study 8B), are carrying out informal sector activities based on the products of modernisation.

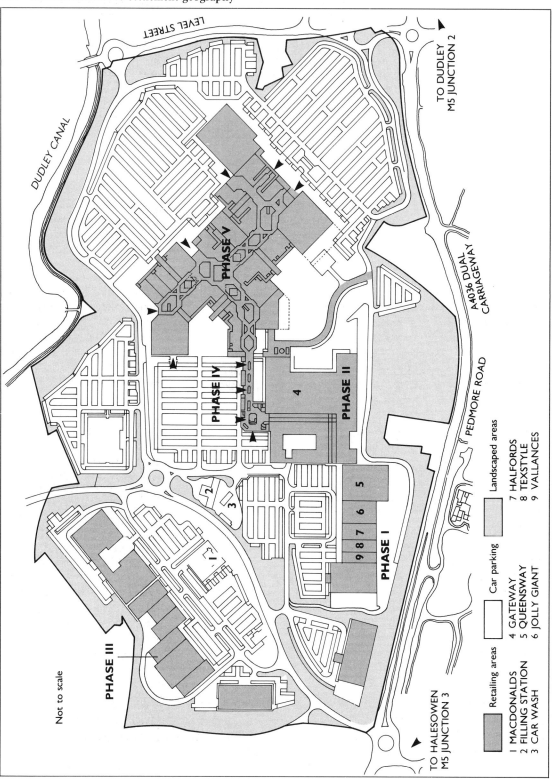

Fig. 8.10 Merry Hill Shopping Centre, Dudley, West Midlands.   *Source: Richardsons Developments Ltd.*

Merry Hill Shopping Centre, Dudley, West Midlands

Merry Hill is a controversial development. Its enlargement from a series of retail warehouses and a superstore into a regional shopping centre of the American type was passed by Dudley Metropolitan District Council by one vote in May 1986. Before and since that date its development has been a matter of concern for planners and retailing organisations in the surrounding region.

When complete, the Merry Hill Centre will provide over 170,000 m² of retailing facilities on a 50-hectare site in the Dudley Enterprise Zone where rates are not payable until the early 1990s and the majority of capital expenditure can be offset against tax. It lies in the heart of the Black Country in the West Midlands conurbation with 230,000 potential customers within a 10-minute drive, 840,000 within 20 minutes and 2 million within half an hour.

The development, which began in 1984, has taken place in five phases (Fig. 8.10). Phases I–IV were completed by late 1986, and phase V opened for trading in late 1989. Phase I comprises 15,000 m² of retail warehousing for firms such as MFI, Halfords and B&Q. The second phase, covering 10,000 m², is a large Gateway superstore with additional specialist foodstores, opticians and clothing and footwear outlets. Phase III, 20,000 m² in area, is also retail warehousing together with a 'Children's World' store, a drive-through Macdonalds, a Pizza Hut

and a 10-screen cinema. Phase IV, providing a further 3,500 m², is a two-level shopping mall with a foodcourt (340 seats) in a glazed atrium. Phases I–IV have 2,700 surface car-parking spaces and are served by a large fleet of minibuses. Phase V, the final phase, provides a further 93,000 m² of shopping facilities in the form of a two-level shopping mall with a major department store, fashion shops, a food court, a 'finance' court and speciality shops. The mall is climatically controlled. When this phase is finally completed there will be 7,000 free car-parking spaces, and a £22m monorail system will operate around the site.

Figure 8.11 shows the four-tier shopping hierarchy in the West Midlands before the opening of the Merry Hill Centre in 1986. At the top of the hierarchy is the central shopping area of Birmingham. Below Birmingham are two subregional centres at Wolverhampton and Coventry. At the third level are the town centres of Dudley, Solihull, Stourbridge, Sutton Coldfield, Walsall and West Bromwich. At the bottom of the hierarchy are 18 district (large suburban) centres. Since late 1986 Merry Hill has been the sixth largest shopping centre in the West Midlands, equivalent to town centres in Dudley or Solihull. When phase V is completed it will rival Wolverhampton at the second tier of the hierarchy.

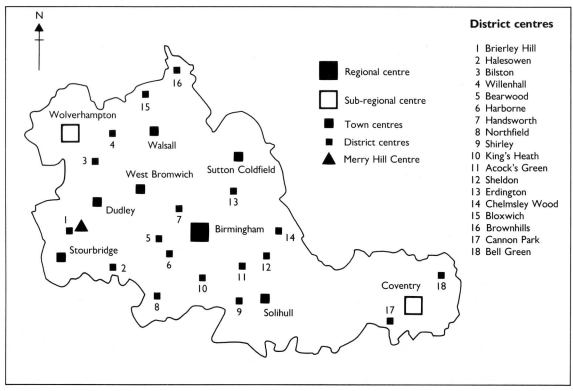

Fig. 8.11 The shopping hierarchy in the West Midlands
prior to the opening of the Merry Hill Centre.
Source: West Midlands Structure Plan, 1980.

How has this development – a sort of 'cuckoo in the nest', as one critic described it – affected the pattern of shopping and shopping provision in the surrounding region? Is it causing existing centres to decline? Is it socially divisive, catering only for middle-class car-owners? If rival centres decline, will there emerge a class of shoppers who are only able to reach impoverished and unattractive centres?

To answer some of these questions an investigation was carried out in the autumn of 1988 to assess the impact of phases I–IV (Burnley, 1989). A total of 240 consumers were interviewed at the Merry Hill Centre, 100 more were interviewed at Dudley, Stourbridge, Wolverhampton, Birmingham and Brierley Hill, and 44 retailers were questioned in Dudley, Stourbridge and Brierley Hill.

Of the 240 shoppers interviewed at Merry Hill, 75 per cent had arrived by car, 12 per cent

by minibus and 7 per cent by the West Midlands bus service. The remaining 6 per cent had walked from nearby residential areas. Seventy-two per cent of the Merry Hill sample had come from within a 4-mile radius, 19 per cent from a zone extending from 4 to 8 miles from the centre, and the remaining 9 per cent from a wide zone extending from 8 to 26 miles from Merry Hill. Unlike many other centres of this type, Merry Hill is not near a motorway and is relatively poorly served by the motorway system. Its impact is therefore likely to be more local than might be expected, and thus its effect on its nearest rivals – Dudley and Stourbridge town centres and Brierley Hill district centre – are likely to be immense.

Burnley found that there had been substantial shop closures in these centres between 1984 and 1988. In 1984 there were 5 vacant shops in Stourbridge town centre; in 1988 there were 13.

In Brierley Hill there had been 1 in 1984; there were 30 in 1988. Only in Dudley town centre was there little change: 6 in 1988 as against 5 in 1984. However, the Dudley figures mask substantial decline. Halfords, MFI, Allied Carpets and W H Smith's 'Do It All' had all gone in the intervening period and Sainsburys and Mothercare were soon to close. The biggest impact was at Brierley Hill where 30 per cent of its shop units were vacant in late 1988, and where 8 out of 12 retailers interviewed reported a decrease in trade. The new Moor shopping precinct at Brierley Hill, opened in 1986, had been extremely badly hit, with a substantial number of unoccupied units and a 'ghost town' atmosphere.

Burnley's study suggests that phases I–IV of Merry Hill have already had a marked impact on shopping centres in Dudley Metropolitan Borough. With the completion of Phase V, the impact on the two town centres of Dudley and Stourbridge is likely to be much greater and the nearest subregional centre at Wolverhampton will also be in direct competition with Merry Hill for the first time. Even without phase V, shoppers at Merry Hill perceived it to be more attractive than the established centres in terms of safety, cleanliness, parking, accessibility and hours of opening. The addition of a department store and other specialist facilities, all set within an attractive, weatherproof environment, look certain to increase its attractiveness to shoppers. In these circumstances there must be a great danger that Dudley and Stourbridge town centres will become no more than 'convenience' shopping centres as high street multiples such as Boots, Littlewoods, Marks and Spencer and BHS re-consider their trading positions and slim their operations or pull out altogether. Nor does the impact stop at retailing organisations. The poorer sections of society and the elderly, especially those living some distance from Merry Hill, may find shopping opportunities and choices diminished in the future, and the environment of the traditional shopping centre may suffer some deterioration.

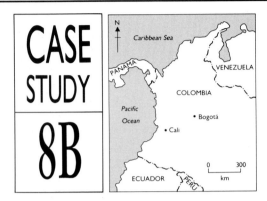

CASE STUDY 8B

Informal economic activity in Colombia: the garbage pickers of Cali

Fig. 8.12 Garbage picker on Smokey Mountain garbage dump, Manila. Hordes of men, women and children work on the dump, seeking to scavenge whatever items they specialise in: bottles, wire, newspapers, plastic bags, clothing, metal cans . . .
Source: United Nations.

Garbage picking is an occupation found throughout the Third World in cities as different as Manila, Marrakesh and Mexico City (Fig. 8.12). It exemplifies many of the problems of the urban poor and yet is part of an economic system that provides a livelihood for numerous people. Birkbeck (1979), in his classic study of garbage pickers in Cali, Colombia, illustrates many of the issues relating to this kind of employment. Cali grew rapidly after 1945 with the development of major paper, non-ferrous minerals, rubber products and electrical machinery industries, but also with many informal industrial activities. By the late 1970s, Cali's population exceeded a million and the municipal authorities were collecting and dumping some 400 tonnes of domestic waste per day.

This domestic garbage formed the raw material from which about 400 garbage pickers made their living by scavenging items from the waste deposited daily by municipal trucks at the city garbage dump. (Another 300 or so worked ahead of the trucks as they went about their collection, taking items from garbage cans brought from homes, in the short time before these were emptied into the trucks. Many others collected waste independently of the municipal system, especially from offices, shops and rich neighbourhoods.) Figure 8.13, though based on only a small sample, indicates the variety of

All figures are given as percentages			
Males	86.5		
Females	13.5		
Age distribution		**Marital status**	
0–15 years	21.6	Single	67.0
16–30 years	32.4	Consensual union	13.5
31–45 years	40.0	Married	13.5
45+ years	5.4	Widowed	5.4
Birthplace		**Residence**	
Cali	55.4	Nothing	12.9
Outside Cali	44.5	Rented room(s)	61.0
		Rented house	6.4
Length of time in job		Own house	9.6
0–3 years	44.0	Other	9.6
4–6 years	14.7		
7–9 years	2.9		
10+ years	38.0		

Fig. 8.13 Some socio-economic characteristics of garbage pickers in Cali, Colombia. *Source*: Birkbeck, 1979.

people involved in garbage picking. Many of these lived in single rooms, renting accommodation in the city centre or in peripheral squatter areas. The number of female workers is much higher in some other areas but the large number of young people is not untypical. Most garbage pickers in Cali specialise in recovering particular materials: paper and cardboard (the most important item), scrap metal, bottles, bones (used in the animal foods industry) or plastics, for example.

The high cost of imported pulp or alternative raw materials for the paper industry of Cali, which manufactures products such as tissues, cardboard and asphalted cardboard roofing tiles, has made it economically worth while to use waste paper. The majority of this is provided by garbage pickers. The system of collection at the time of Birkbeck's study involved one central and several 'satellite' warehouses. The latter were small-scale operations, buying and sorting about a tonne of waste paper per day for transmission to the central warehouse where it was more carefully classified before being sent to the factory. The satellite warehouses bought their paper almost entirely from garbage pickers, often on a fairly regular basis but at prices varying in relation to the quality and quantity of waste paper collected and the individual bargains struck between seller and buyer. In some cases, garbage pickers sold to middlemen who then re-sold material to the warehouses. Such middlemen usually worked together to keep prices paid to the pickers at a low level. Whatever system is employed, the garbage pickers are dependent for their earnings on how hard they work and how much those they sell to are prepared to pay. If they do not work (for illness or other reasons) they do not get paid, and they have no guarantee of continued employment if market fluctuations adversely affect the industry they are supplying with raw materials. In the late 1970s a garbage picker in Cali might expect to earn £1 or so per day (roughly the equivalent of the official minimum wage in Colombia) but had no security, and although playing an important part in a modern industry saw the real profits reaped elsewhere in the system.

The position of garbage pickers in Cali is not much different from that of similar workers elsewhere. The sale of a thousand plastic sacks scavenged from Manila's municipal dump and washed in the sea would earn a garbage picker only about £3 in 1989. A scrap-metal picker in Casablanca might earn a little more than that on a good day, but his 'finds' and his income would probably vary more from day to day. These and many thousands of others may work hard and fulfil a useful role in the economy but gain few rewards for their diligence and enterprise.

9

Planning and the city

Almost every aspect of urban life reflects planning by local, regional or national government, by corporations, by voluntary groups and by individuals. In small and highly urbanised countries, such as Singapore or the Netherlands, attempts at centrally controlled planning are very obvious. This has also been true of the communist countries of Eastern Europe, though political changes at the end of the 1980s are likely to bring about a different situation in future. However, even in countries where central government intervention in urban planning is weak or non-existent, as in the USA, local planning ordinances have a surprisingly significant impact.

Urban planning is multi-faceted. It can involve improving environmental quality, creating employment opportunities, facilitating access to housing, tackling transport problems, improving access to recreation facilities, curbing urban sprawl, and attempting to overcome the problems of unequal and over-urbanisation. Clearly these are not independent of each other and some well-known examples of urban planning adopt a comprehensive approach in order to solve a number of related problems.

Planning of our cities is clearly an important and wide-ranging topic. Four main issues have been selected here for investigation: unequal urban development, urban sprawl, transport problems, and housing in the cities of the Third World.

Primate cities, regional imbalance and urban planning

Primate cities occur in many parts of the world but are more common in the Third World than elsewhere. Their degree of dominance varies but concern has often been expressed that they may inhibit economic growth in other areas by attracting the bulk of investment to themselves, thereby increasing inequalities within a country and probably resulting in a further increase in the primacy ratio (the ratio of the population of the first to the second largest city in a country). The situation tends to be most extreme in relatively small countries such as some of the Caribbean Island states, or in Thailand where Bangkok has more than 40 times as many inhabitants as Chiang Mai, the second city.

Primate cities represent a particular type of uneven urban development within a country, but imbalance between regions in terms of urban development is also common. In Peninsular Malaysia, for example, most large urban centres have developed in the west of the peninsula, the focus of most colonial economic interest being in that area where tin and rubber production were most important. While centres such as Kuala Lumpur, Ipoh and Georgetown grew up in the west, there was no incentive for similar development in the east coast region and government attempts to increase commercial activity in this region since the 1960s have been handicapped by the much higher degree of modernisation and better infrastructure previously developed in the west. Similarly, in Brazil urban and industrial growth was largely concentrated in the São Paulo-Rio region and by 1970 approximately half Brazil's manufacturing employment was in São Paulo state. The focus on export-oriented production in Third World countries has been a major influence on many of these regional concentrations, with urban primacy, often in a coastal city, developing where trade was concentrated through one centre, and a broader regional concentration occurring where several centres were involved.

Spatial patterns of development inevitably change through time and various attempts have been made to generalise about this process, of which *Friedmann's centre-periphery model* (Fig. 9.1) is one of the best known. It incorporates some of the ideas of earlier writers, notably Myrdal and Hirschmann. Friedmann's model has been criticised by many people, including the author himself. Criticisms have included the fact that many Third World countries do not fit the assumption that colonisation occurred in sparsely populated regions; the suggestion that Friedmann gives insufficient emphasis to foreign influences either in terms of their significance in decision-making or their control over economic activities; the tendency to underplay the importance of political attitudes and philoso-

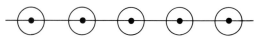

Stage 1

Stage 1 is typified by the existence of a series of small, local centres in a sparsely populated, newly colonised country. New mining and agricultural ventures develop, serviced by small urban centres between which there is little interaction.

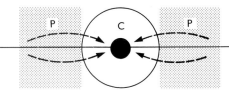

Stage 2

Stage 2 involves early industrialisation and a growing concentration of investment into a single centre or core (C), favourably situated in relation to such features as natural resources, local and foreign markets. Regional disparities increase as resources and people flow to the core region (a process described as 'polarisation' by Hirschmann and 'backwash' by Myrdal), and peripheral areas (P), with stagnating or declining economies, develop. At the heart of the core region, a primate city develops.

Fig. 9.1 Friedmann's centre-periphery model: a sequence of stages in spatial organisation.
Source: Friedmann, 1972.

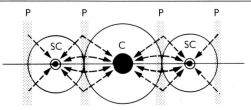

Stage 3

Stage 3 is marked by increasing industrial maturity, and the simple core-periphery structure of stage 2 is replaced by a situation in which secondary centres (SC) develop in the peripheral regions, possibly helped by regional development policies responding to political demands from the periphery. These provincial cities are likely to possess substantial regional markets or significant natural resources. By this stage, people and resources show a greater tendency to flow outwards (Myrdal's 'spread' effect) at the national scale but 'backwash' may be dominant within particular regions so investment is concentrated in a limited number of urban centres. Peripheral areas are reduced in size but still exist between the major national core, still growing and dominated by the primate city, and peripheral or secondary sub-centres.

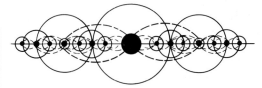

Stage 4

Stage 4 involves a much more complex series of resource movements as a fully integrated national system emerges. In an ideal situation, this combines efficiently located firms, maximum potential for future growth and minimum inter-regional imbalances.

phies; the failure to emphasise the significance of poverty *within* regions and cities; and the assumption that poor countries will necessarily go through a series of stages leading to their becoming 'developed'.

Despite these criticisms, some of the theoretical ideas incorporated in the model have been applied by Third World governments, notably in the form of growth centre policies (see Chapter 4) that have sought to lessen regional imbalances. This has involved investment in urban centres in peripheral regions (often encouraged by financial incentives) with the hope that the benefits of this investment will spread or 'trickle-down' to adjacent rural areas too. Several new capital cities have been established, partly in the hope that they would serve as growth centres away from the previous capitals (for example Dodoma in Tanzania). In some cases, the new capitals have also served other functions, as with Brasilia and Islamabad, both to some extent symbolic of future aspirations for their country. More

general attempts to adopt growth centre policies as a means of spreading economic development in countries such as Chile, Colombia and Kenya have not been particularly successful. Reasons for this include attempts to include a large number of relatively small centres (in the case of Kenya over a thousand 'centres' including many small villages), lack of adequate funding, poor links between centres and their hinterlands, a disregard of institutional/cultural structures and their place in the diffusion of innovations, and the dominance of foreign-based investment in industries that do not serve local needs. Despite the many difficulties associated with growth centre policies, they continue to be widely used in the Third World.

Exercise 9.1

Primate city growth in Mexico

The table below shows various aspects of
population change in Mexico and Mexico City
between 1921 and 1980.

Population growth in Mexico and the Metropolitan Area of Mexico City (MAMC), 1921–80

	1	2	3	4	5	6
	Population		% of national population	Annual rate of growth (prior decade)		% increase due to migration
Year	National ('000s)	MAMC ('000s)		National	MAMC	
1921	14,335	659		n.a.	n.a.	n.a.
1930	16,553	1,043		1.4	4.7	n.a.
1940	19,654	1,553		1.7	4.1	n.a.
1950	25,779	3,419		2.7	7.5	51.2
1960	34,923	5,564		3.1	5.0	38.3
1970	48,377	8,605		3.3	4.4	43.2
1980	67,383	15,082		3.4	5.8	–

n.a. = information not available
Source: Campbell and Wilk, 1986.

a) Complete the table by calculating the percentage of the national population living in Mexico City in the various years (column 3).

b) Construct a diagram to show the data you have entered in column 3.

c) Re-read the second half of Chapter 3 and the first section of this chapter and then suggest reasons why migration (column 6) has played such a large part in the phenomenal growth of Mexico City.

d) One of the measures being taken in developing countries to balance urban growth, is to establish new or enlarged cities in those regions that are economically backward and suffering badly from out-migration. If successful, what will be the benefits of such schemes for:
i) the areas in which the new or enlarged cities are located; and
ii) the primate cities?

e) Why has the type of scheme outlined in (d) rarely been successful in developing countries?

Although primacy is not as marked in industrial countries, it has been a cause for concern in a number of countries for several decades and a variety of solutions have been sought, using 'sticks' (restrictions on development in the largest metropolitan region) or 'carrots' (incentives to invest in provincial cities), or a combination of both.

Urban planning in France

The dominance of Paris in France (it is six times as large as the next biggest city) has long been a bone of contention, and a 1960 plan for the capital proposed a complete stop on its future physical growth. This unrealistic proposal was superseded in 1965 by another plan that assumed a continued 4 per cent annual growth of population, effectively doubling Paris's population in 20 years, but with a deliberate slowing down of the rate of growth that it was assumed would occur if there were no restrictions, in order to promote urban growth in the provinces. The rate of migration was to be checked by channelling government investment into selected provincial cities and encouraging private investment there. Eight major urban agglomerations were selected as *métropoles d'équilibre* (balancing metropolises) to act as counterweights to the pull of Paris (Fig. 9.2). They were also

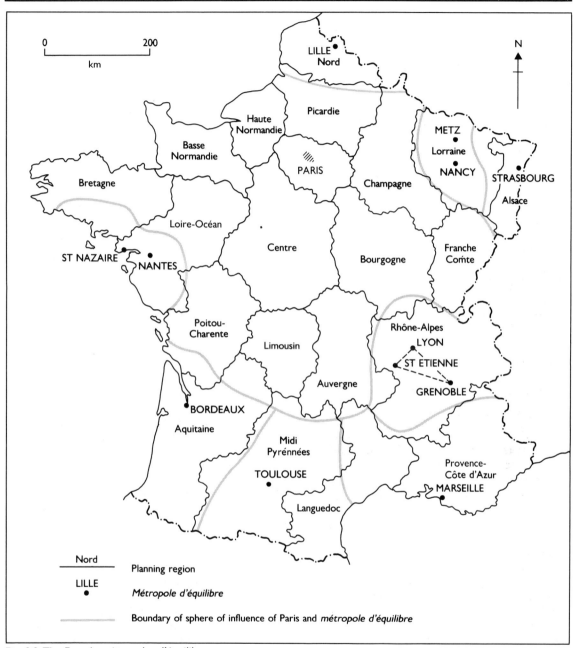

Fig. 9.2 The French *métropoles d'équilibre*.
Source: after Hall, 1974.

designed to act as growth poles in their own regions – a very necessary secondary function in some cases, for example Lille, which lies at the centre of an old and declining industrial area based on coal, steel and textiles, and Lyon-St Etienne-Grenoble, whose surrounding region included a declining coalmining area and marginal hill farming districts on the edge of the Massif Central. Paralleling the planned development of these provincial centres, a number of new cities were created in the outer Paris region, to perform much the same role as the *métropoles*

	% change 1968–75	% change 1975–82
Paris	3.6	−0.5
Lyon	7.5	−0.1
Marseille	5.9	0.9
Lille	5.1	−0.1
Bordeaux	7.5	2.6
Toulouse	14.1	2.5
Nantes	11.8	2.5

Fig. 9.3 Population change 1968–82 in Paris and six *métropoles d'équilibre.*
Source: Ogden, 1985

Fig. 9.4 Assisted areas (1972) and new towns in England and Wales. The map shows government-assisted areas at their greatest post-war extent. Among the new towns, Stevenage, Crawley, Hemel Hempstead, Harlow, Hatfield, Welwyn, Basildon and Bracknell were all early post-war London overspill towns. Milton Keynes, Peterborough and Northampton were designed as second-generation London new towns at greater distances from the capital. Aycliffe, Peterlee, Cwmbran, Skelmersdale, Redditch, Runcorn, Washington, Telford and the Central Lancashire New Town were established outside conurbations and industrial agglomerations to act as growth centres and counter-attractions to London and the South-East.

NEW TOWNS (name and date of designation)	Population (thousands)	
	At designation	Projected total size
1 Stevenage (1946)	7	105
2 Crawley (1947)	9	79
3 Hemel Hempstead (1947)	21	80
4 Harlow (1947)	5	90
5 Hatfield (1948)	9	30
6 Welwyn (1948)	19	50
7 Basildon (1949)	25	134
8 Bracknell (1949)	5	60
9 Aycliffe (1947)	0	45
10 Peterlee (1948)	0	30
11 Cwmbran (1949)	12	55
12 Corby (1950)	16	83
13 Skelmersdale (1961)	10	80
14 Redditch (1964)	32	90
15 Runcorn (1964)	30	90
16 Washington (1964)	20	80
17 Newtown (1967)	6	13
18 Milton Keynes (1967)	44	250
19 Peterborough (1967)	83	187
20 Northampton (1968)	131	260
21 Warrington (1968)	122	202
22 Telford (1968)	70	250
23 Central Lancashire (1970)	250	500

N

0   80
km

Special Development Areas

Development Areas

Intermediate Areas

Derelict Land Clearance Areas

d'équilibre in the provinces, and these have grown very rapidly, thus diminishing the potential impact of the provincial centres.

The results of the 1975 and 1982 French censuses show that although Paris grew much less quickly than its main provincial rivals between 1968 and 1975, a more significant trend was the population decline of Paris and two of the regional centres between 1975 and 1982, and the relative stagnation of the other provincial centres in the same period (Fig. 9.3). This suggests that France's major urban agglomerations have become victims of the counterurbanisation trend that has manifested itself in other parts of Europe and the USA. Greater personal mobility, the decentralisation of industrial and commercial activity and the generally better quality of life found in smaller settlements, which in the main showed healthy growth rates in France between 1975 and 1982, are all influencing population distributions and lifestyles. If the counterurbanisation trend continues then the primacy of Paris may not be the problem it once was; more significantly, channelling investment towards major provincial urban centres in order to equalise growth looks like an outdated strategy.

Planning policies for Britain

Concern about the 'drift to the South' and the 'North-South divide' with urban stagnation and decline in the North and economic prosperity and growth overwhelmingly concentrated in London and the South-East region, has caused successive British governments to put into operation a whole series of economic and urban policies designed to decentralise investment and revive the ailing economies of the conurbations outside the Midlands and the South-East. These have been motivated by a variety of considerations including a desire to spread prosperity as widely as possible across the nation, to improve the quality of life in depressed urban-industrial districts, and to ease the problems of congestion, pressure on land for development, and escalating house prices in the South-East.

Figure 9.4 shows the parts of England and Wales that at one time or another since 1945 have received government subsidies as part of regional policy for new industrial and office buildings, new plant and machinery, and capital

loans for industrial expansion schemes. For much of the same period, economic development in the South-East has been restricted by the use of *industrial development certificates* (IDCs) which the government could withhold in congested areas or those which it regarded as having sufficient industrial development already. Office developments were also restricted in the 1960s and 1970s by the use of office development permits (ODPs). More recently, *enterprise zones* (where development unrestricted by planning regulations, free of local rates and eligible for 100 per cent capital allowances for buildings is allowed), and *urban development corporations* (government-funded semi-independent development agencies), have been introduced to encourage economic growth and diversification in the old industrial heartlands. Additionally, since 1946, 10 new towns have been established outside the major provincial English conurbations to act as growth centres and counter-attractions to London and the South-East (Fig. 9.4). Unfortunately, since the mid-1970s they have been held partly responsible for inner-city decline and since that time have attracted much less investment than previously.

Despite these measures, economic growth remains firmly concentrated in the South-East and adjacent parts of East Anglia and the South-West. The populations of the major English provincial population centres of the West Midlands, Merseyside, Greater Manchester, Tyne and Wear, and of Clydeside in Scotland, all fell between 1971 and 1985 and are expected to continue to do so until the end of the century. On the other hand it is forecast that London, which experienced population decline in its inner and outer boroughs between 1971 and 1981, will cease to lose population between the mid-1980s and the end of the century, as gentrification of inner areas, aided by such schemes as the London Dockland Development Corporation, more than offset any counterurbanisation trends.

Urban sprawl and its containment

If cities grow in an uncontrolled way then diseconomies and disadvantages are an inevitable outcome. In the cities of the developed world, uncontrolled growth results in long journeys to work, traffic congestion, heavy pollution and, for inner-city dwellers, long journeys to urban fringe

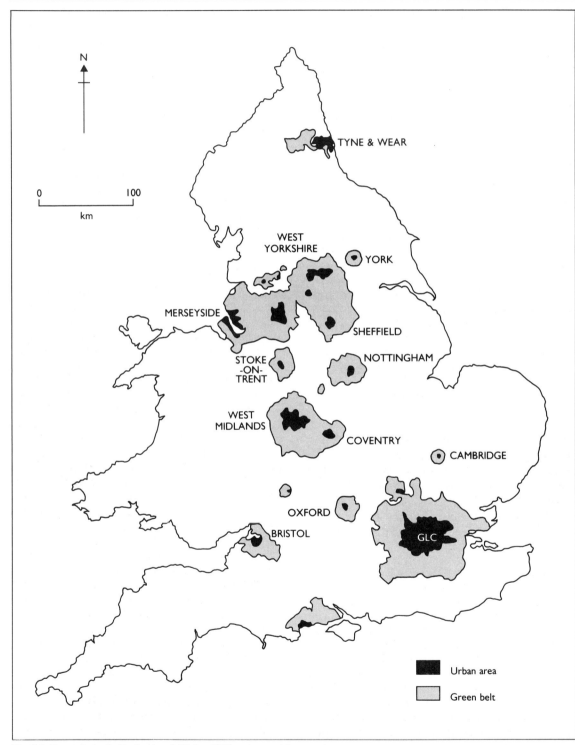

Fig. 9.5 Green belts in England and Wales 1986, approved by statute.
Source: Munton, 1986.

countryside. In less developed countries where expansion is taking place most rapidly, housing, traffic, water supplies, telecommunications and electricity services are subject to frequent breakdown because the existing infrastructure is unable to cope, and scarce resources make improvement and expansion of systems virtually impossible. One possible solution to the problem, as we have seen, is to attempt to *deconcentrate* urban growth; another is to contain it.

Containment measures in the UK

One of the best-known attempts at *urban containment* is that pursued in England and Wales based on *green belts*. A green belt is essentially a collar, which can be many kilometres wide, in which non-agricultural or non-recreational developments are severely restricted. Green belts thus shape or preserve the general pattern of urban growth, arrest outward expansion, prevent coalescence of neighbouring urban areas, and preserve accessible urban fringe countryside for public enjoyment. They may help too in the resuscitation of inner areas by restricting the supply of peripheral development land. They also have disadvantages. For example, they restrict the supply of development land, thus raising land prices and causing high housing densities. Nor do green belts, as was suggested by their originators, serve as recreation spaces for populations throughout the urban areas constrained by them. There are 25,000 ha of public open space in London's green belt, but it is mostly used by local people. Despite these criticisms there are now 15 approved green belts in England and Wales covering more than 1.75 million hectares (Fig. 9.5).

The green belt idea in the UK is linked to the concept of *new towns*: new or enlarged existing centres designed in part to act as *overspill centres* beyond the green belt. The idea has been particularly well developed around London where, between 1946 and 1949, eight new towns were designated close to the capital (see Fig. 9.4). These early new towns were followed in the late 1960s by three additional new towns, at Northampton, Peterborough and Milton Keynes, at a much greater distance from the capital. Although the new town programme is widely recognised as an outstanding planning achieve-

ment, some criticisms have been levelled at the towns. First, it has been alleged that they have tended to be selective in terms of in-migration so that inner-London residents have been under-represented. Secondly, they have consumed a disproportionate amount of public money that could, say the critics, have been better used to improve inner-city neighbourhoods. Thirdly, the first generation of new towns have not become as self-contained as their advocates suggested they would, and have therefore increased rather than decreased commuting to the capital. In spite of these and other criticisms, and the shortcomings of green belts, the urban containment strategy for London has became a model for urban planners in other parts of the world.

Randstad Holland

A quite different urban containment problem is found in the Netherlands, a small but highly urbanised country. The largest towns and cities in the Netherlands lie in a loose horseshoe shape with a diameter of 50–60 km in the west of the country, running from Dordrecht westwards to Rotterdam, up the North Sea coast through The Hague, Leiden and Haarlem, then east and south-east though Amsterdam to Utrecht. This polynuclear conurbation has become popularly known as Randstad Holland (Fig. 9.6). In 1980 it contained about 43 per cent of the country's population on about 17 per cent of the land area. Randstad means 'round city', and the unique feature of the conurbation is that unlike others it has a rural core or *green heart* containing small towns, villages and farmland.

By the early 1970s decentralisation of population in the Netherlands was taking place at such a pace that the major centres of Randstad were in decline, the green heart was being rapidly suburbanised and medium- and long-distance commuting to work in Randstad was rapidly expanding. To counter these trends a number of related policies were introduced in the mid- and late-1970s. First, it was proposed that popula-tion dispersal, which had earlier been encour-aged, should be strictly controlled by increasing the residential capacity of the existing towns and cities in Randstad through urban renewal and infilling. In this way it was hoped that urban spread and commuter congestion would be curtailed. It was further proposed that any

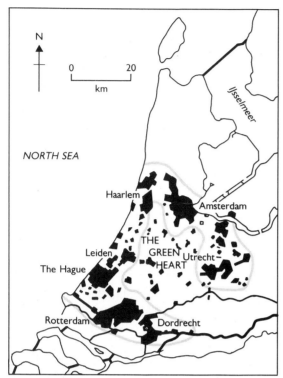

Fig. 9.6 Randstad Holland, 1980.
Source: Information and Documentation Centre for the Geography of the Netherlands, 1980.

dispersal that did take place should be channelled to growth towns and growth centres, some of the latter being in Randstad itself. Thirdly, seven buffer zones, which were already in existence to prevent the coalescence of neighbouring urban areas, were given a more positive role as recreation areas, with land being acquired, laid out and managed by the central government. Lastly, non-agricultural developments in the green heart were to be carefully controlled.

Urban containment in the Third World

Urban containment strategies are also beginning to appear in plans for the rapidly growing cities of the Third World. In Cairo, for example, with a population of more than 10 million estimated to rise to 20 million by the end of the century, residential densities in some of the poorest districts are over 2,000 per hectare, cemeteries have been colonised by squatters, and urban spread is taking place along all the main arteries into the city. In its ambitious 1970 master plan

for the city, the government proposed a system of five satellite towns in order to deconcentrate urban growth. Little progress has been made, however, because of financial problems, difficulties in attracting employment to such sites, and because their isolated locations (two are on the edge of the Western Desert), mean that they are detached from agricultural hinterlands where they would have occupied valuable farmland but within which they might have been expected to act as counter-magnets to Cairo.

An equally ambitious scheme was published in 1981 to contain urban spread in the federal district that contains Mexico City. This city stretches 40 km from north to south and 20 km east to west. It is expected to expand from its 1980 population of 15 million to 31 million by

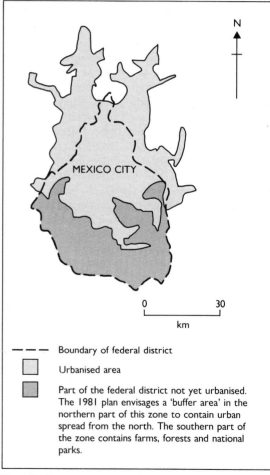

```
- - - -   Boundary of federal district

[  ]      Urbanised area

[▨]       Part of the federal district not yet urbanised.
          The 1981 plan envisages a 'buffer area' in the
          northern part of this zone to contain urban
          spread from the north. The southern part of
          the zone contains farms, forests and national
          parks.
```

Fig. 9.7 Urban containment planning in the federal district containing Mexico City.

the end of the century. If this growth is uncontrolled, the city would eventually spread over the remaining semi-urbanised areas in the south of the federal district (Fig. 9.7). The plan envisages a buffer area surrounding the city's southern periphery, to contain urban spread in that direction. The buffer area will retain its rural character dominated by intensive agriculture, public parks and other recreational areas. Beyond the buffer zone the remainder of the federal district, which contains farms, forests and national parks, is designated as a conservation area in which urban growth will not be allowed.

Urban transport planning issues

The relentless growth of major cities and their commuting hinterlands, the increasing use of trucks for the movement of goods, the growing separation of place of residence and place of work, and, in the developed world, high levels of car ownership, have all placed immense pressures on urban road systems. The obvious answer is simply to build more roads and to increase the capacity of existing ones, but this has often resulted in a *congestion cycle* in which the problem is merely increased (Fig. 9.8), as recent experience on the London orbital motorway, the M25, has shown.

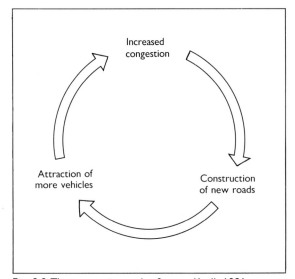

Fig. 9.8 The congestion cycle. *Source*: Krell, 1981.

Transport systems

For this reason, a number of new ideas have been introduced and systems already well-established in some cities have been taken up elsewhere. Among these are the introduction and extension of underground and surface railway systems, monorails, supertrams, bus-only lanes, bus gates, dial-a-bus systems, park-and-ride and tidal-flow road systems.

Surface railways are the oldest cheap and relatively fast method of moving large numbers of urban residents between home and work, and they continue to carry large numbers of commuters. London's surface railway system carries three-quarters of a million passengers a day, and Tokyo's copes with an incredible 20 million. Underground systems are not a new idea either. London's network dates from the 1860s and is still being extended. Other well-developed underground systems operate in New York, Paris, Tokyo and Moscow. Moscow's underground, for example, extends over 216 km and is used daily by more than 7 million passengers. Recent years have seen a number of completely new urban railway systems incorporating underground, surface and elevated sections, including the Newcastle Metro, and the London Docklands light railway, the San Francisco and Atlanta rapid transit systems in the USA, and the mass rapid transit systems of Hong Kong and Singapore.

The Newcastle Metro is Britain's first integrated public transport system linking buses with a new 'supertram' system, and was opened in 1980 at a cost of £200 million. The supertram network, much of it unwanted British Rail line, covers 55 km and runs on the surface in the suburbs and at the coast, but underground in the central area. The Metro's advantages are its speed, comfort and relative cheapness. It has greatly eased the movement of workers and shoppers into the centre of Newcastle and has relieved congestion on road crossings on the River Tyne. It is also pollution free.

Another well-known but less successful scheme is the so-called Bay Area Rapid Transit (BART) scheme centred on San Francisco. This 120 km scheme, on which construction began in 1962, was to be of the highest comfort and sophistication, with expensively carpeted, air-conditioned trains, operated by computers, gliding noiselessly between stations of the highest architectural standard. It was designed mainly to carry commuters to the centre of San Francisco and Oakland. The network was opened to the first passengers in 1972, having already cost over £1.6 billion. However, the Californian commuters were loath to give up their cars, and this, combined with low levels of use outside office hours, meant that five years later it was still only carrying slightly over half of its expected passenger load and was making a heavy loss, which put a considerable load on local ratepayers.

The performance of BART has made planners and politicians in cities both inside and outside the USA, especially where there are many car users, wary of large capital projects and has caused them to consider a variety of other smaller-scale schemes. Park-and-ride, for example, has found acceptance in some British towns and cities where the demand for access to the centre by car is greater than can be coped with or is considered desirable. Park-and-ride schemes involve car users from the urban periphery and beyond who work or shop in the central area in parking their vehicles in designated car parks well outside the centre and taking a bus for the remainder of the journey. This allows the use of cars and buses in conditions to which they are best suited: cars in the low-density suburbs and surrounding countryside where bus services may be relatively infrequent, and buses along busy urban corridors where demand for movement is high but car-parking space scarce or expensive.

Oxford: transport policies

Oxford, as well as being a university town with a high-density historic core containing over 1,000 listed buildings, is also a large regional shopping and entertainment centre and a major tourist attraction. In the last 20 years in particular it has experienced major congestion and parking problems. As part of the City Council's 'Balanced Transport Policy' it introduced its first park-and-ride interchange at Redbridge in 1973 to cater for motorists driving from outside the city (Fig. 9.9). It was opened at the height of the Christmas shopping season with parking for 250 cars and minimal bus fares. It was widely publicised in the local press and on local radio

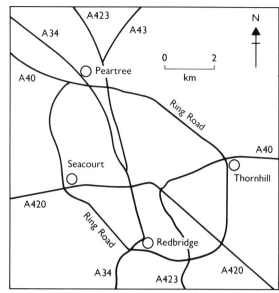

Fig. 9.9 Park-and-ride interchanges in Oxford.
Source: Gardiner, 1989.

and was a huge success. By 1988 car parking at Redbridge had been increased to 970 cars, and additional park-and-ride interchanges had been opened at Seacourt (1974), Peartree (1976) and Thornhill (1985). There are now over 3,000 car parking spaces at the four interchanges. At peak times (7.00 am – 9.00 am) on weekdays over 600 cars per hour enter the interchanges and on Saturday mornings over 550 cars per hour use them. An unpublished survey (Gardiner, 1989) has shown that during a typical weekday before 9.00 am, 76 per cent of interchange users are using the park-and-ride scheme to commute to work, and the remaining 24 per cent to shop in the central area. After 9.00 am the position is reversed with 81 per cent of users being shoppers. On a typical Saturday morning only 2.8 per cent of users are commuters and 85 per cent are shoppers.

Planning for Third World housing improvement

Various problems associated with Third World urban housing provision have already been mentioned in earlier chapters. In many Third World cities, 25 to 50 per cent of the population live in housing that is substandard by conventional planning measures. Most of this is in decaying city centres or informal settlements.

Housing problems cannot be solved in isolation, however, and improvements in employment, service provision and social facilities are also crucial if lifestyles are to be enhanced and people are to be able to afford better housing. Singapore (Case Study 9) provides one of the few examples of a Third World country that has successfully resolved most of its housing problems through strong government action. In many other cases government involvement in attempts to solve housing problems has been limited or unsuccessful.

Some early government schemes proved dramatic failures. A much publicised development in Caracas, Venezuela, carried out by Banco Obrero, the main official housing agency, at the instigation of President Jimenez, aimed to replace extensive squatter settlements (*ranchos*) by so-called 'super-blocks'. In Caracas, 85 high-rise (mostly 15-storey) super-blocks were constructed between 1954 and 1958 with a further 12 in the nearby port of La Guaira. The Caracas blocks alone housed nearly 160,000 people, most of them from *ranchos* demolished with scarcely any warning, a move that caused considerable resentment. Public participation in the planning process was virtually non-existent. By 1958, when Jimenez was overthrown, the situation was in near-chaos. The hastily built super-blocks had numerous design faults, many residents could only afford to pay rent by illegally sub-letting rooms in their apartments, scarcely any maintenance work was carried out, some 4,000 squatters had occupied empty flats, green space between the blocks had been occupied by informal housing, crime was widespread, and some blocks were in the hands of political extremists. Few of the planned social facilities had been provided, so community integration was difficult and only about half the schools needed had been built. This scheme clearly emphasises the problems that can arise in providing high-technology, Western-style housing in Third World countries without very careful planning and community involvement in the planning process.

Housing policies in Tunis

A study of housing needs and policies in the Tunisian capital, Tunis, by Lawless (1986), provides a more general view of a fairly typical situation in a Third World city. The Muslim city of Tunis had been in existence for over a thousand years when French colonial control was established in the late 19th century. Thereafter a planned European settlement was constructed adjacent to the traditional Arab quarter, the *medina*, with the later addition of extensive European suburbs and a modern industrial zone – a pattern typical of many colonial cities. No plans were made for Tunisian residential development, however, despite rapid in-migration especially from the 1940s until independence in 1956. As the *medina* became grossly overcrowded, informal housing (*gourbivilles*) developed, largely self-built, initially of earth construction but later of more permanent materials, and mainly sited in marshy areas not wanted by Europeans. Thus before independence, the European-controlled planning system effectively ignored the needs of the Tunisian population. Some 150,000 Europeans (one-third of the city's 1956 population) emigrated after independence but were rapidly replaced by more wealthy Tunisians moving out of the *medina* into the former European areas where, Lawless suggests, they quickly adopted European value systems. Their former homes in the *medina* were soon occupied and usually subdivided by new in-migrants and refugees from *gourbivilles* destroyed by early government 'degourbification' programmes.

Since independence, government housing policies have encouraged private construction either for direct purchase or by a system of rent-purchase that enables houses to be bought over a period of 15–20 years with money lent at low interest. Both these approaches are beyond the means of most urban dwellers. 'Popular cities' have been built by the main state housing organisation (SNIT) and municipalities but even these have generally proved too expensive for low-income groups, requiring monthly payments of at least 30 dinars, when some two-thirds of the urban population had average monthly incomes of less than 50 dinars. The urban poor remain crowded into the *medina* and the *gourbivilles*, while two-thirds of the city's residential area is occupied by less than one-third of its people. Recent economic policies creating new growth centres in Tunisia may slow the flood of in-migrants to Tunis but will not solve the problems of present low-income residents.

Self-help schemes

Situations like that in Tunis are very common. So what is the way forward for planners and people? There is no single, easy answer to this question. The urban poor are a large and immensely varied group of people living in many different circumstances. Singapore's approach (Case Study 9) will not be appropriate in most cases. Recently, emphasis has been given to the view that most low-income urban residents are resourceful and, given encouragement and security of tenure, will improve their homes by self-help processes. Governments can help by providing basic amenities, economic opportunities and social services. Perceived needs vary, however, and both types and results of self-help approaches may be widely divergent.

The most basic form of aided self-help is in upgrading existing low-income housing. In Bangkok, where much of the poorest housing is in swampy, ill-drained areas, government investment has mainly been in all-weather walkways, land drainage and water supply. In the Tondo foreshore area of Manila, formerly the site of the Philippines' largest squatter settlement, similar improvements have been supplemented by the provision of individual land titles, providing a degree of security that is difficult to achieve in Bangkok because of the complex private land ownership situation. Increased security may also lead to increased costs, however, particularly for low-income residents who rent their homes. In some cases, as in Nairobi's Mathare Valley (Chapter 5), greedy landlords in informal housing areas have perhaps benefited most from attempts to legalise land-holdings.

'Sites and services' and 'core housing' schemes provide alternatives to the upgrading of existing housing, aiming to provide new homes at relatively low cost with subsequent improvement being anticipated when occupants can afford this. *Sites and services schemes* provide basic public services such as roads, water supply and sewerage to an area where plots are available for self-help building; *core housing schemes* involve the addition of a partly finished house to the basic service provision, with the occupant expected to construct additional rooms. The World Bank and other international agencies have often helped with the funding of such

schemes since the 1970s. Despite this, finances have often been inadequate to make ideal use of these schemes and frequently they have been occupied by middle- rather than low-income families. A very large core housing scheme at Dandora, east of the Mathare Valley in Nairobi, had by 1987 provided homes for about 100,000 people but most of these were not the poorest of Nairobi's urban dwellers for whom the scheme was originally designed. A major reason for this was the insistence of various planning authorities on achieving certain building standards for both the 'core' and other elements of the houses, that inevitably increased building costs. A much smaller sites and services scheme at Morogoro in Tanzania provides evidence of similar problems (Exercise 9.2).

Clearly, self-help programmes, even with 'outside' assistance of the kinds provided in core housing or sites and services schemes, are not a simple or complete answer to the problems of low-income housing. Moreover, some writers have argued that such schemes provide a good excuse for Third World urban authorities to put only limited resources and effort into housing the urban poor while waiting for the latter to solve their own housing problems. Perhaps much more fundamental changes in political and/or economic attitudes are necessary before there can be major housing improvements in most Third World cities.

Exercise 9.2

Housing the low-income poor: Morogoro, Tanzania

Study carefully the information and map provided concerning a sites and services project in Tanzania, and then answer the questions that follow.

Morogoro was one of the five cities selected for inclusion in the Second National Sites and Services project (1976–81) in Tanzania. An analysis of the development there has been made by Materu (1986). The World Bank provided about 40 per cent of the funding but the project began three years late (1979) in Morogoro because of the delays in receiving the funds, shortage of other finances, and administrative difficulties. The project was designed to provide for overspill population

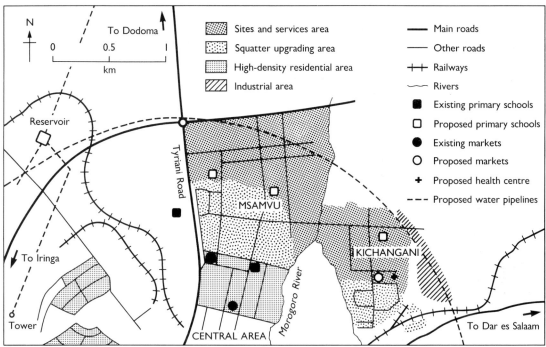

Source: Materu, 1986

from nearby squatter areas and other low-income households. Upgrading of the squatter areas was also planned. Meetings of council officials with squatters indicated that some squatters would be displaced by upgrading schemes providing roads, drainage ditches and piped water, but house-owners (not tenants) would be given compensation and offered a plot on the sites and services scheme. It was also emphasised that houses in the sites and services scheme would have to comply with building regulations, and rents and service charges would have to be paid. Security of tenure would be given to those remaining in the 'squatter' areas but they would have to begin to pay land rent and service charges when upgrading was completed. No squatting would be allowed outside the present area occupied. Those unable to comply with the new charges were advised to go back to rural areas or find accommodation with friends. This 'consultation' caused considerable antagonism to the developments.

Approximately 600 plots, each 12 m × 24 m, were developed in the sites and services project by the mid-1980s, some 200 fewer than originally intended because of waterlogging

problems in Msamvu and competition with industrial land uses in Kichangani. Although the project was intended for low-income residents, the council tended to give priority to rather more affluent applicants with regular employment, so more than half the plots were occupied by people with incomes well above the level originally intended. The relatively low standards of infrastructure provision in both squatter and sites and services areas – a result mainly of financial constraints – have also caused problems, some of which have been exacerbated by the limited community support for and involvement in the development of the schemes. Drainage ditches have been blocked with debris, pit latrines have caused problems in Msamvu which has a high water table, and there is under-provision of water standpipes causing delays and shortages. Attempts to provide cheap building materials for those constructing homes in the sites and services area have been hampered by shortages of suitable materials, while financial loans to assist such people have been hampered by complicated application procedures. Finally, the limited number of new job opportunities in Morogoro has caused certain problems for people in both the former squatter areas and the sites and services project area.

Consider both the information provided above and in the text as a whole in attempting the following:

a) Discuss the implications for residents in the Morogoro squatter areas of the information given them by the council before upgrading began. Why would this cause 'considerable antagonism'? Explain what kinds of residents were probably most badly affected by the new developments.

b) It has been suggested that larger plots of land than those provided in the sites and services scheme would have been economically advantageous to the occupants. Explain why this may be so.

c) What would encourage the council to 'give priority to rather more affluent applicants with regular employment' for sites and services plots?

d) In what ways might greater community involvement in the Morogoro developments have helped?

e) Discuss how the failure to create more new jobs in Morogoro in the 1980s would hamper progress on the sites and services project.

f) On the basis of wider reading, suggest why sites and services schemes in Tanzania, like that at Morogoro, have usually been handicapped by financial shortages.

Planning housing provision in Singapore

As recently as 1960, Singapore suffered from many of the problems of urban overcrowding and inadequate housing provision that are still typical of cities in most developing countries today. Singapore's situation has since changed dramatically, however, largely as a result of the activities of the Housing and Development Board (HDB) which has been responsible for the construction and management of low-cost public housing since 1960 and more recently has taken control of other public housing schemes, to become the sole national public housing authority in Singapore.

Singapore City had its origins in 1819 when Sir Stamford Raffles laid claim, on behalf of the East India Company, to land near the Singapore River.

Early growth focused on the river, with Raffles responsible, in 1822, for initiating a planned layout for the city that involved separation of the different groups already resident (see Fig. 5.6). The city's population grew rapidly, exceeding 50,000 by 1850, 230,000 by 1900 and 1 million by 1950. Much of this increase was due to migration, mostly from southern China, and from an early stage Singapore's population was dominated by people of Chinese origin. (By the late 1980s, 76 per cent of the 2.7 million people were Chinese in origin, 15 per cent Malay, 6.5 per cent Indian and nearly 2.5 per cent 'other'.) From early times, the central area of the city was largely occupied by shophouses which, as population increased, became dramatically overcrowded, as described by Kaye (see Fig 7.6). In the 19th century European residents began to move out of the central area to more attractive sites further west, a trend followed by other affluent Singaporeans later. Lower-income groups saw few opportunities to improve living conditions in the central area slums, and by the 1930s squatter housing had begun to develop around the fringes of the city and on vacant spaces within the city centre, behind and on top of shophouses, alongside the railway, in swampy areas and on river banks. Some squatter homes were built from traditional rural building materials, others of whatever waste materials were available. Provision of water supplies, sewerage and refuse disposal facilities was haphazard or non-existent in most cases.

From 1927 onwards some public housing was provided by the Singapore Improvement Trust. By 1959 the under-funded Trust had built 27,000 homes, mostly after 1947, housing about 9 per cent of Singapore's population. With the achievement of internal self-government in 1959, a much higher priority was given to housing provision and the HDB began its housing programme in 1960. At this time probably a quarter of a million people occupied the shophouse slums in the city centre, with at least as many people in squatter settlements in the city. The HDB programme, initially designed to provide for the housing needs of the lowest-income groups, has been based on a

	Target	Completed	Percentage of population in public housing at end of period
1960–65	51,000	54,000	25
1966–70	62,000	64,000	35
1971–75	100,000	114,000	45
1976–80	125–150,000	155,000	67
1981–85	*90–105,000		
	**155,000	180,000	81
1986–90	127,000	approx. 100,000 (mid-1988)	approx. 86 (mid-1988)

* original estimate
** revised

Fig. 9.10 Residential units built by HDB, Singapore.
Sources: Singapore HDB annual reports and other official publications.

series of five-year plans supported not only by government subsidies but also by government assistance through land acquisition and clearance, infrastructural provision and resettlement policies. Most low-income families made their living in the city centre where potential building land was limited and expensive. Because of this, early HDB schemes were on the fringes of the city centre (within 6 to 8 km, or half an hour's travelling time) and took the form of high-rise blocks of flats utilising very little land. Flats were small and cheaply constructed, and initially kitchen and toilet facilities were shared. Estates were planned on the neighbourhood concept developed in European new towns with shops, primary schools, clinics and other facilities provided, but this modern approach was complemented by attempts to encourage the maintenance of close kinship ties and traditional Asian community life wherever possible. Contrary to many expectations, the HDB target of 50,000 dwellings in the first five-year plan was exceeded, a pattern repeated in every subsequent plan (Fig. 9.10). Much of the central area was gradually cleared of shophouses with high-rise estates replacing these, though early plans to demolish all the shophouses in the central area have been modified (Figs 9.11 and 9.12)

Not everyone welcomed the new housing. Clearance of squatter houses and dilapidated

▲ Fig. 9.11 Modern development in central Singapore. This complex of shops (lower floors) and housing has in part replaced the shophouses of Upper Nankin Street described by Kaye (see Fig. 7.6). The high-rise housing is typical of much of that which has been built in the central area HDB estates.

▼ Fig. 9.12 Shophouses in central Singapore, late 1980s. Early plans to demolish this kind of housing throughout the central area have given way in some areas to attempts to renovate existing housing by refurbishing both interiors and exteriors and providing improved services (water supply, electricity, sewerage, etc.). Such schemes are still in progress but the availability of alternative housing has reduced population pressures in these areas dramatically. One reason behind the change in policy is the attraction of such areas to tourists visiting Singapore.

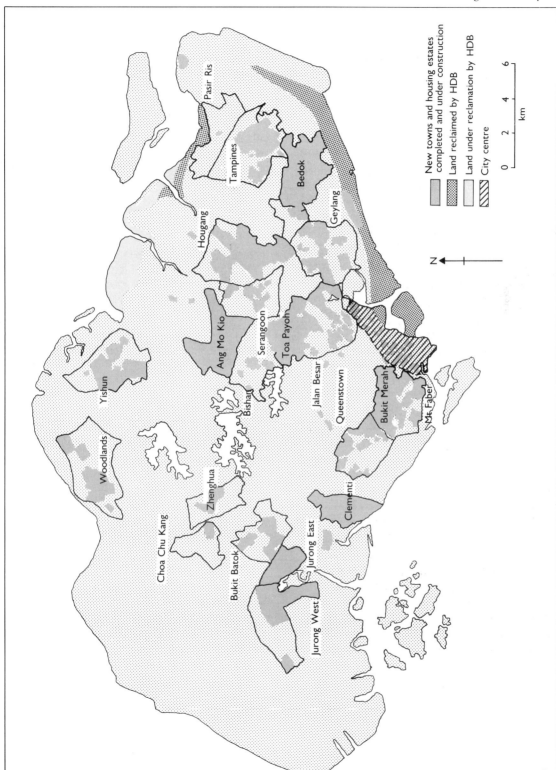

Fig. 9.13 Location of new towns and housing estates in Singapore. *Source:* Singapore HDB annual reports.

shophouse areas meant that their inhabitants were uprooted and often had to change their lifestyle even though provided with new homes; hawkers in the city centre lost many of their customers and landlords lost their source of income. Nevertheless, with full independence achieved in 1965, the government re-affirmed its commitment to the housing programme, to urban renewal and to squatter removal. Gradually, high-rise housing became widely accepted, the quality of the accommodation built improved and by 1970 the housing needs of the lowest-income groups had largely been met. The HDB now turned its attention more to middle-income groups who were finding it difficult to compete in the private housing market. By this time, the initial emphasis in public housing on providing homes to rent had altered. Home ownership schemes were introduced in 1964, and by 1970 applications to purchase flats exceeded applications to rent for the first time, a pattern maintained ever since. Purchase has been facilitated by the government allowing Singaporeans to use money paid into the Central Provident Fund (basically a pension fund to which employees and their employers contribute) for making repayments for their home purchase.

In addition to building housing estates (normally housing 10,000–50,000 people), work began in the 1960s on the first *new towns* (housing 125,000–250,000 people). Early new towns such as Toa Payoh (Fig. 9.13) were close to the city, but most are further away with Woodlands, projected to house 250,000 people, being over 20 km from the city. The new towns have good access to the centre by road and the partially completed Mass Rapid Transit railway. Within the new towns there is a range of light industries and other employment opportunities, and each new town has a wide range of facilities and services in the town centre plus a number of

smaller neighbourhood centres each serving some 20,000 people. Most current housing development is in the new towns.

During the 1970s and 1980s the HDB sought to meet the needs of an ever-widening range of people. The design of flats progressively improved, largely on the basis of consultations with representatives of the inhabitants. Increasingly the focus has been on providing larger flats with better amenities. During the 1980s the HDB also took over control of the HUDC (Housing and Urban Development Company) flats, designed to be more spacious and better equipped than HDB flats but, like them, subsidised by the government. Increasing attention has also been given to providing a pleasanter environmental setting for the high-rise blocks, with more green space around them.

Thus the situation has changed in 30 years or so from one in which the principal aim was to provide cheap but sound housing near the city centre for low-income families to one in which good homes are provided in environmentally pleasant surroundings for most of Singapore's people in a variety of locations throughout the island (Fig 9.13). In the process of this change, city-centre slums and squatter settlements have been eradicated, the city centre largely re-developed, transport systems and the general infrastructure dramatically improved, and over 86 per cent of Singapore's population provided with public housing, more than three-quarters of these owning their homes. Two major factors have contributed to these impressive achievements: the government's determination to ensure the success of their housing policies by every means available, and the rapid economic development of Singapore. Few other countries with comparable housing problems in 1960 have had the benefit of *either* of these factors during the 30 years since then.

Bibliography and further reading

This severely selective bibliography includes both sources that are specifically referred to in the text, and some suggestions for further reading within the general field of study.

Chapter 1

Champion, A.G. (1989) 'Counterurbanisation in Britain', *Geographical Journal*, 155, 52–59.

Cloke, P. (1977) 'An index of rurality for England and Wales', *Regional Studies*, 11, 31–46. (1979) *Key Settlements in Rural Areas*, Methuen, London. (1985) 'Counterurbanisation: a rural perspective', *Geography*, 70, 13–23.

Dwyer, D.J. (1979) 'Urban geography and the urban future', *Geography*, 64, 86–95.

Fielding, A.J. (1989) 'Migration and urbanisation in Western Europe since 1950', *Geographical Journal*, 155, 60–69.

Herington, J. (1984) *The Outer City*, Harper and Row, London.

Keeble, D. (1989) 'The dynamics of European industrial counterurbanisation in the 1980s: corporate re-structuring or indigenous growth?', *Geographical Journal*, 155, 70–74.

Mountjoy, A.B. (1986) 'The progress of world urbanisation', *Geography*, 71, 246–48.

Pacione, M. (1984) *Rural Geography*, Harper & Row, London.

Phillips, D.R. and Williams, A. (1984) *Rural Britain: A social geography*, Blackwell, Oxford.

Smailes, A.E. (1971) 'Urban systems', *Transactions of the Institute of British Geographers*, 53, 1–14.

Weekley, I. (1988) 'Rural depopulation and counterurbanisation: a paradox', *Area*, 20, 127–34.

Chapter 2

Allerston, P. (1970) 'English village development: findings from the Pickering district of North Yorkshire', *Transactions of the Institute of British Geographers*, 51, 95–109.

Beresford, M.W. and St Joseph, J.K.S. (1979) *Medieval England – an aerial survey*, 2nd edition, Cambridge University Press, Cambridge.

Chisholm, M. (1968) *Rural Settlement and Land Use*, 2nd edition, Hutchinson, London.

Cloke, P. (1979) *Key Settlements in Rural Areas*, Methuen, London.

Dawson, A.H. (1975) 'Are geographers indulging in a landscape lottery?' *Area*, 7, 42–45.

Elkins, T.H. (1962) *Germany*, Chatto and Windus, London.

Hoskins, W.G. (1988) *The Making of the English Landscape*, New edition, Hodder and Stoughton, London.

Hudson, V.L. (1977) 'Suburbanisation: An investigation of rural settlement patterns in the Lincoln area'. Unpublished undergraduate dissertation, Sheffield City Polytechnic.

Ooi Jin Bee (1976) *Peninsular Malaysia*, Longman, London.

Roberts, B.K. (1987) *The Making of the English Village*, Longman, London.

Royal Commission on the Historical Monuments of England (1987) *Houses of the North York Moors*, HMSO, London.

Taylor, C. (1983) *Village and Farmstead*, Philip, London.

Thorpe, H. (1964) 'Rural settlement', in J.W. Watson and J.B. Sissons, *The British Isles: A Systematic Geography*, Nelson, London.

Wibberley, G.L. (1972) 'Rural activities in rural settlements' (paper presented at Town and Country Planning Association Conference).

Chapter 3

Blunden, J. and Curry, N. (1988) *A Future for Our Countryside*, Blackwell, Oxford.

Bromley, R.D.F. and Bromley, R. (1982) *South American Development: A Geographical Introduction*, 2nd edition, Cambridge University Press, Cambridge.

Clout, H.D. (1972) *Rural Geography: An Introductory Survey*, Pergamon, Oxford.

Connell, J. (1974) 'The metropolitan village', in J.H. Johnson, *Suburban Growth*, 77–100, Wiley, London.

Ghate, R. (1978) 'Generation gap in an Indian village', *Geographical Magazine*, 50, 580–86.

Grove, A.T. and Klein, F.M.G. (1979) *Rural Africa*, Cambridge University Press, Cambridge.

Jones, G. (1973) *Rural Life*, Longman, London.

King, R. (1980) 'Land consolidation in Cyprus', *Geography*, 65, 320–24.

Lea, J. (1988) *Tourism and Development in the Third World*, Routledge, London.

Mabogunje, A.L. (1980) *The Development Process: a spatial perspective*, Hutchinson, London.

Newby, H. (1980) *Green and Pleasant Land*, Penguin, Harmondsworth.

Odell, P.R. and Preston, D.A. (1978) *Economies and Societies in Latin America: a geographical interpretation*, 2nd edition, Wiley, Chichester.

Pacione, M. (1980) 'Differential quality of life in a metropolitan village', *Transactions of the Institute of British Geographers*, 5, 185–206.

Slee, B. (1987) *Alternative Farm Enterprises*, Farming Press, Ipswich.

Spencer, J.E. (1977) 'The transformation of the traditional rural village', in R.C. Eidt, K.W. Singh and R.P.B. Singh (eds), *Man, Culture and Environment*, Kalyani, New Delhi.

Thomas, C. and Vojvoda, M. (1973) 'Alpine communities in transition: Bohinj, Yugoslavia', *Geography*, 58, 217–26.

Thorpe, H. (1951) 'The influence of inclosure on the form and pattern of rural settlement in Denmark', *Transactions of the Institute of British Geographers*, 17, 113–29.

Chapter 4

Bradford, M.G. and Kent, W.A. (1977) *Human Geography: theories and their implications*, Oxford University Press, Oxford.

Bromley, R.D.F. and Bromley, R. (1988) *South American Development: A Geographical Introduction*, 2nd edition, Cambridge University Press, Cambridge.

Cherry, G.E. (1976) *Rural Planning Problems*, Leonard Hill, London.

Cloke, P. (1979) *Key Settlements in Rural Areas*, Methuen, London.

Clout, H.D. (1972) *Rural Geography: an introductory survey*, Pergamon, Oxford.

Cohen, J.M. and Isaksson, N.-I. (1987) Villagisation in Ethiopia's Arsi Region', *Journal of Modern African Studies*, 25, 435–64.

Coppock, J.T. (1977) *Second Homes: Curse or Blessing*, Pergamon, Oxford.

Doherty, J. (1987) 'Tanzania: twenty years of African socialism 1967–1987', *Geography*, 72, 344–48.

Eden, M.J. (1978) 'Ecology and land development: the case of Amazonian rainforest', *Transactions of the Institute of British Geographers*, 3, 444–63.

Haywood, I. (1985) 'Settlement planning and developing countries: the Gezira experience in Sudan', *Ekistics*, 52, 332–37.

Hirst, M. (1978) 'Recent villagisation in Tanzania', *Geography*, 63, 122–25.

Lea, D.A.M. and Chaudhri D.P. (eds) (1983) *Rural Development and the State*, Methuen, London.

Leeming, F. (1985) *Rural China Today*, Longman, New York.

Luling, V. (1989) 'Wiping out a way of life', *Geographical Magazine*, 59(7), 34–37.

Mabogunje, A.L. (1980) *The Development Process*, Hutchinson, London.

Madeley, J. (1986) 'Ethiopia's new villagers', *Geographical Magazine*, 58(5), 246–49.

Meijer, H. (1981) *Zuyder Zee/Lake IJssel*, Information and Documentation Centre for the Geography of the Netherlands, Utrecht/The Hague.

Moran, E.F. (1981) *Developing the Amazon*, Indiana University Press, Bloomington.

Moseley, M.J. (ed.) (1978) *Social issues in Rural Norfolk*, Centre for East Anglian Studies, University of East Anglia, Norwich.

Nyerere, J.K. (1967) *The Arusha Declaration*, Government Printer, Dar-es-Salaam. (1977) *The Arusha Declaration: ten years after*, Government Printer, Dar-es-Salaam.

Pacione, M. (ed.) (1983) *Progress in Rural Geography*, Croom Helm, London.

Peake, H. (1922) *The English Village*, Benn, London.

Shaw, J.M. (1979) *Rural Deprivation and Planning*, Geo Books, Norwich.

Shucksmith, D.M. (1983) 'Second homes: a framework for policy', *Town Planning Review*, 54(2), 174–93.

Stacey, M. (1985) 'The social and economic effects of second homes in the Yorkshire Dales'. Unpublished undergraduate dissertation, Sheffield City Polytechnic.

Sutton, K. (1982) 'Socialist villages of Algeria', *Third World Planning Review*, 4, 247–64.

Trautmann, W. (1986) 'Algeria: the agrarian revolution and the system of state-directed co-operatives', *Ekistics*, 53, 213–23.

Chapter 5

Brunn, S.D. and Williams, J.F. (1983) *Cities of the World*, Harper & Row, New York.

Carter, H. (1981) *The Study of Urban Geography*, 3rd edition, Edward Arnold, London. (1983) *An Introduction to Urban Historical Geography*, Edward Arnold, London.

Griffin, E. and Ford, L. (1980) 'A model of Latin American city structure', *Geographical Review*, 70, 435–47.

Hake, A. (1977) *African Metropolis: Nairobi's self-help city*, Chatto and Windus, London.

Lee-Smith, D. and Memon, P.A. (1988) 'Institution development for delivery of low-income housing', *Third World Planning Review*, 10, 217–38.

McGee, T.G. (1967) *The South-east Asian City*, Bell, London.

Morgan, W.T.W. (ed.) (1967) *Nairobi: city and region*, Oxford University Press, Nairobi.

O'Connor, A. (1983) *The African City*, Hutchinson, London.

Smailes, A.E. (1955) 'Some reflections on the geographical description and analysis of townscapes', *Transactions of the Institute of British Geographers*, 21, 99–115. (1964) 'Towns' in **J.W. Watson and J.B. Sissons** (eds), *The British Isles: A Systematic Geography*, Nelson, London. (1966) *The Geography of Towns*, Hutchinson, London.

Chapter 6

Berry, B.J.L. (1981) *Comparative Urbanisation*, Macmillan, London.

Berry, B.J.L. and Rees, P.H. (1969) 'The factorial ecology of Calcutta', *American Journal of Sociology*, 74, 445–91.

Boal, F.W. (1976) Ethnic residential segregation', in **D. Herbert and R. Johnston** (eds), *Social Areas in Cities*, Volume 1, Wiley, London.

Doherty, P. (1989) 'Ethnic segregation levels in Belfast', *Area*, 21, 151–59.

Drakakis-Smith, D. (1987) *The Third World City*, Methuen, London.

Harris, C.D. and Ullman, E.L. (1959) 'The nature of cities', in **H.M. Mayer and C.F. Kohn** (eds), *Readings in Urban Geography*, University of Chicago Press, Chicago.

Herbert, D.T. (1972) *Urban Geography: A Social Perspective*, David & Charles, Newton Abbot.

Hoyt, H. (1939) *The Structure and Growth of Residential Neighbourhoods in American Cities*, Federal Housing Administration, Washington DC.

Jones, E. and Eyles, J. (1977) *An Introduction to Social Geography*, Oxford University Press, Oxford.

Knox, P. (1982) *Urban Social Geography: An Introduction*, Longman, London.

Murdie, R.A. (1969) *Factorial Ecology of Metropolitan Toronto 1951–1971*, University of Chicago Press, Chicago.

Park, R.E., Burgess, E.W. and Mackenzie, R.D. (1925) *The City*, University of Chicago Press, Chicago.

Paterson, J.H. (1975) *North America*, 5th edition, Oxford University Press, London.

Poole, M.A. and Boal, F.W. (1973) 'Religious residential segregation in Belfast in mid-1969: a multi-level analysis', in **B.D. Clark and M.B. Gleave** (eds), *Social Patterns in Cities*, IBG, London.

Radford, J.P. (1979) 'Testing the model of the pre-industrial city: the case of ante-bellum Charleston, South Carolina', *Transactions of the Institute of British Geographers*, 4, 392–410.

Robson, B. (1975) *Urban Social Areas*, Oxford University Press, London.

Rule, S.P. (1989) 'The emergence of a racially mixed residential suburb in Johannesburg: demise of the Apartheid city?', *Geographical Journal*, 155(2), 196–203.

Shaw, M. (1977) 'The ecology of social change: Wolverhampton 1851–71', *Transactions of the Institute of British Geographers*, 2, 332–48.

Short, J.R. (1984) *An Introduction to Urban Geography*, Routledge & Kegan Paul, London.

Sjoberg, G. (1960) *The Pre-Industrial City*, Free Press, Glencoe, Illinois.

Chapter 7

Adams, J.S. (1969) 'Directional bias in intra-urban migration', *Economic Geography*, 45, 302–23.

Bassett, K. and Short, J.R. (1980) *Housing and Residential Structure*, Routledge & Kegan Paul, London.

Dicken, P. and Lloyd, P.E. (1981) *Modern Western Society: A Geographical Perspective on Work, Home and Well-Being*, Harper & Row, London.

Drakakis-Smith, D. (1987) *The Third World City*, Methuen, London.

Dwyer, D.J. (1975) *People and Housing in Third World Cities*, Longman, London.

Gilbert, A. and Gugler, J. (1982) *Cities, Poverty and Development: Urbanisation in the Third World*, Oxford University Press, Oxford.

Johnston, R.J. (1971) *Urban Residential Patterns: An Introductory Survey*, Bell, London.

Johnstone, M.A. (1979) 'Urban squatters and unconventional housing in Peninsular Malaysia with special reference to small cities', *Tropical Geography*, 49, 19–33. (1983) 'Housing policy and the urban poor in Peninsular Malaysia', *Third World Planning Review*, 5, 249–71.

Kabagambe, D. and Moughtin, C. (1983) 'Housing the poor: a case study in Nairobi', *Third World Planning Review*, 5, 227–48.

Kaye, B.(1960) *Upper Nankin Street, Singapore*, Oxford University Press, Singapore.

McBride, N. (1988) 'An investigation of the distance-decay function in the migration to selected areas of Bristol'. Unpublished undergraduate dissertation, Sheffield City Polytechnic.

Mason, P. (1989) 'A study of intra-urban mobility in Sheffield'. Unpublished undergraduate disseration, Sheffield City Polytechnic.

Morgan, B.S. (1976) 'The bases of family status segregation: a case study of Exeter', *Transactions of the Institute of British Geographers*, 1, 1976, 83–107.

Peach, C. (ed.) (1975) *Urban Social Segregation*, Longman, London.

Short, J.R. (1978) 'Residential mobility in the private housing market in Bristol', *Transactions of the Institute of British Geographers*, 3, 1978, 533–47.

Skinner, R.J. and Rodell, M.J. (eds) (1983) *People, Poverty and Shelter: Problems of Self-help Housing in the Third World*, Methuen, London.

Turner, J.F.C. (1968) 'Housing priorities, settlement patterns and urban development in modernising countries', *Journal of the American Institute of Planners*, 33, 167–81.

Williams, D. (1975) 'Jakarta's kampungs', *Architectural Design*, 6, 339–43.

Chapter 8

Association of American Geographers (1973) *The South: A Vade Mecum*, AAG, Washington DC.

Berry, B.J.L. (1963) *Commercial Structure and Commercial Blight*, University of Chicago, Chicago.

Birkbeck, C. (1979) 'Garbage, industry and the "vultures" of Cali, Colombia', in R. Bromley and C.Gerry (eds) *Casual Work and Poverty in Third World Cities*, Wiley, Chichester.

Bromley, R. (1980) 'Municipal versus spontaneous markets? A case study of urban planning in Cali, Colombia', *Third World Planning Review*, 2, 205–32.

Bromley R. and Gerry C. (eds) (1979) *Casual Work and Poverty in Third World Cities*, Wiley, Chichester.

Burnley, S. (1989) 'The Merry Hill Centre (Dudley Enterprise Zone) and its effects on existing retail centres'. Unpublished undergraduate dissertation, Sheffield City Polytechnic.

Daniel, P.W. (1975) *Office Location: An Urban and Regional Study*, Bell, London.

Davies, R.L. (1976) *Marketing Geography with Special Reference to Retailing*, Methuen, London.

Dawson, J. (ed.) *Retail Geography*, Croom Helm, London.

Geertz, C. (1963) *Peddlers and Princes: Social change and economic modernisation in the Indonesian towns*, University of Chicago Press, Chicago.

Guy, C.M. (1980) *Retail Location and Retail Planning in Britain*, Gower, Farnborough.

Husain, M.S. (1980) 'Office relocation in Hamburg: The City-Nord Project', *Geography*, 65, 131–34.

ILO (1972) *Employment, Incomes and Equality: A strategy for increasing productive employment in Kenya*, ILO, Geneva.

Lawless, P and Brown, F. (1986) *Urban growth and change in Britain: an introduction*, Harper & Row, London.

McGee, T.G. and Yeung, Y.M. (1977) *Hawkers in South-east Asian Cities: Planning for the Bazaar Economy*, International Development Research Centre, Ottawa.

Potter, R.B. (1982) *The Urban Retailing System*, Gower, Aldershot.

Santos, M. (1979) *The Shared Space: the two circuits of the urban economy in underdeveloped countries*, Methuen, London.

Chapter 9

Campbell, T. and Wilk, D. (1986) 'Plans and plan-making in the Valley of Mexico', *Third World Planning Review*, 8, 287–313.

Cox, K.R. (1979) *Location and Public Problems*, Blackwell, Oxford.

Davies, C.S. (1983) 'The imprint of federal policy on evolving urban form', in J.W. House (ed.), *United States Public Policy: A Geographical View*, Oxford University Press, Oxford.

Eng, T.S. (1986) 'New towns planning and development in Singapore', *Third World Planning Review*, 8, 253–71.

Eng, T.S. and Savage, V.R. (1985) 'Singapore landscape: a historical overview of housing change', *Singapore Journal of Tropical Geography*, 6, 48–63.

Friedmann, J.P. (1972) 'The spatial organisation of power in the development of urban systems', *Development and Change*, 4, 12–50.

Gardiner, N.I. (1989) 'Park and ride schemes: the Oxford experience'. Unpublished undergraduate dissertation, Sheffield City Polytechnic.

Gilbert, A. and Gugler, J. (1982) *Cities, Poverty and Development: Urbanisation in the Third World*, Oxford University Press, Oxford.

Hall, P. (1974) *Urban and Regional Planning*, Penguin, Harmondsworth. (1981) *Great Planning Disasters*, Penguin, Harmondsworth.

Hartshorn, T.A. (1980) *Interpreting the City: An Urban Geography*, Wiley, New York.

Holcomb, B. (1988) 'Metropolitan development', in P.L. Knox et al, *The United States: A Contemporary Human Geography*, Longman, London.

Johnston, R.J. (1980) *City and Society*, Penguin, Harmondsworth. (1982) *The American Urban System: A Geographical Perspective*, Longman, London.

Krell, K. (1981) *Techniques of Improving Urban Conditions by Restraints on Road Traffic*, OECD, Paris.

Lawless, R. (1986) 'Housing needs and policies in Tunis', *Ekistics*, 53, 157–61.

Lee-Smith, D. and Memon, P. (1988) 'Institution development for delivery of low-income housing', *Third World Planning Review*, 10, 217–38.

Lim, W.S.W. (1984) 'Public housing and community development in Singapore', *Ekistics*, 307, 319–27.

Materu, J. (1986) 'Sites and services projects in Tanzania: a case study of implementation', *Third World Planning Review*, 8, 121–38.

Meijer, H. (1980) *Randstad Holland*, Information and Documentation Centre for the Geography of the Netherlands, Utrecht/The Hague.

Munton, R.J. (1983) *London's Green Belt*, Allen & Unwin, London. (1986) 'Green Belts: the end of an era?', *Geography*, 71, 206–14.

Ogden, P.E. (1985) 'Counterurbanisation in France: the results of the 1982 population census, *Geography*, 70, 24–35.

Pacione, M. (ed.) (1981) *Urban Problems and Planning in the Developed World*, Croom Helm, London.

Singapore Housing and Development Board *Annual Reports*, HDB/Singapore.

Index